W9-CAT-297

No. 555
$8.95

MAJOR APPLIANCE
REPAIR GUIDE

By Wayne Lemons & Bill Price

TAB BOOKS
Blue Ridge Summit, Pa. 17214

FIRST EDITION

FIRST PRINTING—JULY 1971
SECOND PRINTING—MAY 1972
THIRD PRINTING—JANUARY 1974
FOURTH PRINTING—JANUARY 1976

Copyright © 1971 by TAB BOOKS

Printed in the United States
of America

Reproduction or publication of the content in any manner, without express permission of the publisher, is prohibited. No liability is assumed with respect to the use of the information herein.

Hardbound Edition: International Standard Book No. 0-8306-1555-5

Paperbound Edition: International Standard Book No. 0-8306-0555-X

Library of Congress Card Number: 70-162406

Preface

Major home appliance repair is a booming field for an enterprising individual. Not only is the number of such appliances increasing in each home, but the number of homes has been increasing rapidly. All this represents a lucrative potential for the person who equips himself with the know-how to repair our increasingly complex home labor-saving devices.

That is the purpose of this book—to present as much detail as possible on troubleshooting and repair of a variety of today's major appliances. We've covered all categories, using typical models to illustrate essential techniques. With this knowledge, and the application of reason, anyone with average ability should be able to get started in this profitable venture. Some of the material will be quite simple to those with an understanding of electricity, but we felt it necessary to include enough basic information to acquaint the beginner with a good foundation to build on.

Also, where appropriate, you'll find time saving troubleshooting charts which provide clues to the most common troubles in easy to-read tabular form. With diligent effort toward absorbing the material in the following chapters, you should be prepared to embark on a money-making and satisfying adventure!

Wayne Lemons
Bill Price

Contents

1 GENERAL TROUBLESHOOTING PROCEDURES   7
Make Sure You Have Found the Trouble

2 TOOLS, TESTERS & EQUIPMENT   15
Volt-Ohmmeters—Using the Ohmmeter—The Clip-On Ammeter—Motor Capacitor Checker—Motor Start Box— Finding Leaks—Snifter Valves—Line-Tap or Saddle Valves—Connecting Tubing

3 ELECTRIC MOTORS   42
Checking Bearings—Motor Speeds

4 BASIC REFRIGERATION SYSTEM   54
The Compressor—The Condenser—Capillary Tube— Evaporator—Refrigeration Gas—Thermostat—The Refrigeration Cycle—Refrigerators—Where Troubles Occur—Checking the Refrigerant—Checking For Leaks— Removing Breaker Strips—Replacing Refrigerator Door Gaskets — Replacing Freezer Door Gaskets — Door Latches

5 ELECTRICAL TROUBLES IN REFRIGERATORS & FREEZERS   120
Unit Doesn't Run—Starting The Compressor Motor Manually—Using a Starter Box—Motor Starting Relays— Overload Protectors—Capacitors—Changing Thermostats—Condenser Fan Motors

6 DISHWASHERS   148
Portable & Built-In Dishwashers—Leaking Around Door Gasket—Timer—Heating Element—Drain Inoperative— Motor Starting Relays—Solenoid Valves—Impeller

7 AUTOMATIC WASHERS   **166**
The Timer—The Wash Cycle—The Spin Cycle—Rinse
Cycle—Pumps—Transmissions—Out-Of-Balance Switch
—Water Valves—Water Level Controls—"Suds Savers"

8 DRIERS   **199**
Installing a Drier—Electrical Troubleshooting—Motor
Doesn't Run—Wiring Diagrams—Timers—Door Switch-
es—Temperature Selector Switch—Thermostats

9 WATER HEATERS   **226**
Installing a Water Tank—Servicing a Water Tank—Water
Heaters Trouble Chart

10 GARBAGE DISPOSERS   **242**
Mounting — Switching — Drain Connection — Servicing —
Disposer Troubleshooting.

11 ELECTRIC RANGES   **264**
Range Wiring—Checking Burners—Oven Elements—
Timers — Built-In Ranges — Troubleshooting — Electric
Range Trouble Chart

Chapter 1

General Troubleshooting Procedures

No matter what the appliance, it is foolhardy to approach the repair of it without some preliminary and general checks to find out if there really is a fault or if it is just "cockpit" trouble. For example, always be sure to check that power is available at the receptacle and that the appliance is plugged in properly. For 220-volt circuits, this means checking both sides of the line between each "hot" wire and ground for 110 volts and also checking between the two "hot" terminals for 220 volts.

It is not necessary that the voltage be exactly 110 volts or 220 volts and you will seldom find that it is. Most appliances will still operate normally with as little as 105 volts or up to 125 or 130 volts on the nominal 110-volt line; consequently, they'll work normally with between 110 to 260 volts on lines nominally rated at 220 volts. Appliances with motors are more apt to give trouble if the voltage is low, since the motors have difficulty reaching operating speed or at least getting up to speed quickly enough; therefore, a motor may blow a fuse or circuitbreaker when line voltage is low, especially if under a heavy starting load. When overload protector throw-out is a problem, check for low line voltage. It can also happen if the voltage is high to the extreme. You can check power line voltages with an AC voltmeter, with a neon tester (Fig. 1-1), or with test lamps (Fig. 1-2). For 220-volt lines you should have two 110 volt lamps connected in series if you use test lamps for checking, or you may be able to obtain a 220-volt lamp.

Make sure that all switches or timers are properly set. If a timer has preset features for turning the appliance off and on, make sure to check that the timer is in the "manual" position for making tests. Also, check for fuses inside the equipment itself. It is not uncommon for fuses to be hidden inside compartments or behind panels in ranges, driers, even washers. Often an appliance, such as a drier, or dishwasher, will not start until the door is tightly closed. A defective door switch or a door switch bracket that is bent out of shape so that closing the door does not activate the switch can cause such appliances to be inoperative.

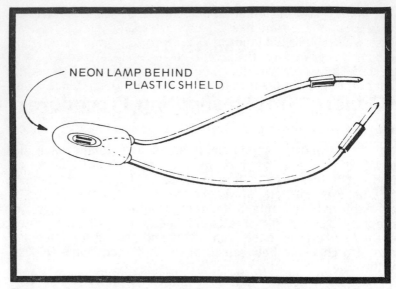

Fig. 1-1. Neon test lamp gives a reliable indication of line voltage by the brilliance of the lamp.

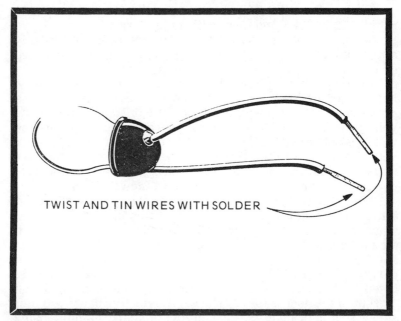

Fig. 1-2. An ordinary incandescent bulb and pigtail socket makes a suitable test lamp.

Listen to the customer's complaint. He or she has "lived" with the appliance and likely knows most of its idiosyncrasies. Listen closely for the fault that the customer wants corrected, otherwise you may find yourself chasing windmills unnecessarily. Once you have determined beyond reasonable doubt that the trouble is in the "inside" of the appliance, then be sure that you disconnect the power plug before starting to remove panels to get inside for tests. Often, removing a panel may let some other part drop down into a "hot" circuit or across "hot" terminals. **Play it safe!**

A good thing to carry with you on any service call is both a 110-volt and a 220-volt extension cord. This will let you apply power as necessary with the appliance moved away from the wall where it is accessible. It may be necessary to make up more than one 220-volt extension cord so as to fit the various kinds of 220-volt receptacles; for example, range and drier receptacles are usually different types. Dishwashers working on 220 volts may have still another type.

When disconnecting wires on a timer, switch or elsewhere, be sure to mark the wires so you know where they belong. There are several ways to do it and you may devise your own way, just so it works for you. Plastic numbers with adhesive backing are now available for marking wires. Some technicians use white adhesive tape to wrap around the wire and a ball point pen to mark the terminal number or letter

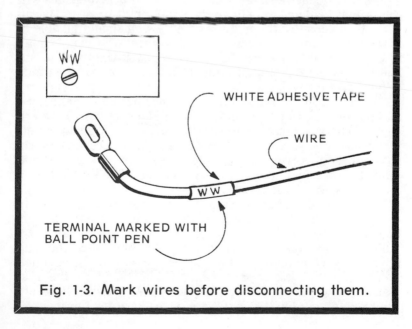

Fig. 1-3. Mark wires before disconnecting them.

from which it came, as illustrated in Fig. 1-3. Others use plastic safety pins and a tag to mark the leads while some use small tags on a string tied to the wire. If two wires come from the same terminal, it is simpler to tie or tape both together and mark once. But whatever you do, don't take off the wires and expect to remember where they go; you might be able to remember for a short while, but if you have to order a part you will almost surely forget how the wires go unless they're marked. Some appliances have the wires marked already, so that you do not have to do your own marking, but make sure you understand the system before using it.

MAKE SURE YOU HAVE FOUND THE TROUBLE

One of the most common mistakes made by a new technician or repairman is the tendency to jump to conclusions not supported by all the evidence. For example, one day you may find that replacing a timer cured a peculiar trouble, so the next day when finding a somewhat similar trouble you jump to the conclusion that this trouble is also a defective timer. Don't risk the embarrassment caused when a replacement part fails to alleviate the trouble. Make sure, then, that you have found the trouble beyond reasonable doubt—don't "convict" a part without making sure all available evidence is in. Just like detective work, the clues will sometimes lead you to believe the exact opposite of the truth. If the trouble is in a timer, for example, you should be able to bypass the timer switch with a jumper wire for a long enough interval to make sure that the timer really is the trouble. But again, make sure that the trouble is not just because the timer is incorrectly set.

If the motor on some appliance does not run, make sure that power is getting to it, and if it is, make sure that there are no overload reset buttons that have popped out and not reset. Make sure, also, that the motor is free to turn—perhaps a gear box is locked. Never turn a motor pulley or pull on a V-belt with the appliance plugged in—people lose fingers and even hands this way. Don't risk it!

A trouble should be repeatable; that is, you should be able to recreate the same trouble, using the original part or hookup. If you can "cause" the same trouble, for instance, by pulling a plug connection apart after you had found the plug apparently not making good connection, then you can be much more sure that the apparent bad connection was the real trouble; however, if pulling the plug apart does not recreate the trouble, you likely should look elsewhere for the trouble.

Do not expect any trouble to cure itself! It happens so seldom that you can almost say it never happens. Sometimes you may start probing around and suddenly the appliance starts working. This does not mean you have fixed the trouble and you can just about bank on its recurrence 98 percent of the time. The moral: Don't probe aimlessly. It is just as easy to check carefully. Look for loose connections at each terminal, but don't just blindly start "jiggling" wires around in the hopes that you will "hit" on the trouble. You may temporarily correct the truublo and not know it, so you will be unable to charge what you should for your sorvices and you can almost be positive of a callback to "lick your calf over."

Take a few minutes to familiarize yourself with the circuit, if one is available. A few minutes ascertaining the "philosophy" of the designer will pay for itself in the hours saved in unstructured diagnosis. Don't be embarrassed by having the customer show you to turn on the equipment. Ask her to go through the regular process so that you can see just where she is having the trouble. This will let you familiarize yourself with unfamiliar switches and may even quickly point the way to a possible solution to the problem. And don't forget that this flatters the owner to "show" you that she has done everything as it should be done. Don't feel belittled to ask the customer for all the information possible. She doesn't know it, of course, but she may have the secret to the problem and you can save yourself a lot of grief by listening carefully to what even an overtalkative customer says.

For example, the customer may indicate that the trouble occurs only at certain times during the day and you may be aware that during that particular time of day there is an excessive load on the power lines in that area, which causes low line voltage and could be the cause of the trouble. Use a small "Down 10" transformer (a test transformer that drops the power line voltage by 10 volts for checking) to see if you can duplicate the customer's trouble. If you can, the problem may indeed be low voltage. Figs. 1-4 and 1-5 show how you can connect a discarded TV power transformer so that it will step the voltage up or down. The idea is to connect the 6.3-volt and 5-volt windings (or another 6.3-volt filament winding) so that this voltage is either subtracted or added to the line voltage as desired. A transformer connected in this manner is called an "autotransformer."

When first checking the transformer windings, it is a good idea to use an AC voltmeter to find the right connections. First, connect one of the 6.3-volt windings in an arbitrary way with the primary winding to see if the output voltage is up or

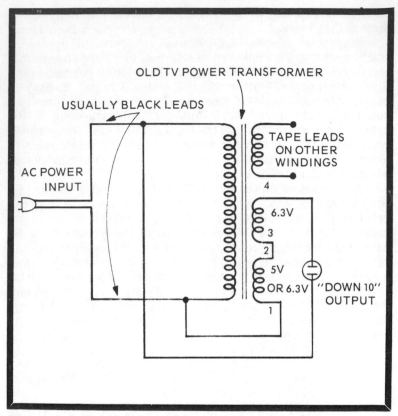

Fig. 1-4. A TV power transformer connected to provide a line voltage 11 to 12 volts lower than the existing line.

down. If it is "up" and you want it "down," then reverse the two lead windings. The normal color code for the windings of a transformer are black leads on the primary or 110-volt winding, green leads for a 6.3-volt winding and yellow for 5-volt windings, but this will vary from manufacturer to manufacturer, so voltmeter testing is the only sure method. The high-voltage winding of the transformer (which are usually red leads) is not used and the leads should be taped so they can't touch.

Practice using your equipment. An ohmmeter is an excellent test instrument, but it must never be used when power is applied to the circuit of the appliance. Always unplug the appliance from the power line before using an ohmmeter. Remember, when checking continuity with an ohmmeter, that at least one of the terminals you are testing should have no other lead from the circuit connected to it, otherwise the test may not be valid.

Regardless of how large this book would be, within any practical limits it would be impossible to cover all the different makes and models of major appliances. We have tried to cover typical examples of the various appliances and the basic theory behind their operation. Obviously, it is up to you as a repairman or technician to make judgments on the spot concerning the different mechanical layouts of appliances. In one case, for example, you may need to pull the back of a drier to get to the controls, while on another the top may pull forward and then lift up. You can usually recognize an appliance with a lift-up top by a seam near the top. Most lift-up tops have to be shoved sharply forward or backward to release hidden catches, but in most cases you will need to remove at least a couple of screws which lock the top in place to prevent accidental disassembly during normal use or shipment.

Finally, always be on the lookout for easier ways to do repairs. Learn to use the tools you have and don't hesitate to

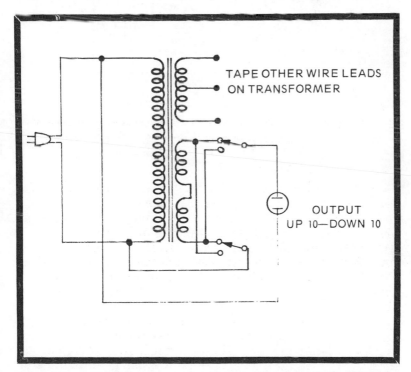

TAPE OTHER WIRE LEADS
ON TRANSFORMER

OUTPUT
UP 10—DOWN 10

Fig. 1-5. A DPDT switch added to the circuit in Fig. 1-4 raises as well as lowers the line voltage.

13

buy other tools or equipment which will help you do a quicker, easier, or better job. But don't depend on your tools or test equipment to do your thinking for you. It has been rightly said that the best technician can do the job with the simplest tools, but he is even better when he has the right tools. In other words, the right tools or equipment won't make you a technician—only your own ingenuity can do that!

Chapter 2

Testers, Tools & Equipment

One of the most useful testers is an ohmmeter which can be used for measuring continuity (whether wires are together or continuous). A basic ohmmeter is simply a meter that indicates current flow, a limiting resistor, and a battery for a power source. Fig. 2-1 is a simple ohmmeter circuit. The meter and resistor R are selected so that when the test leads are connected together the meter will read exactly full scale.

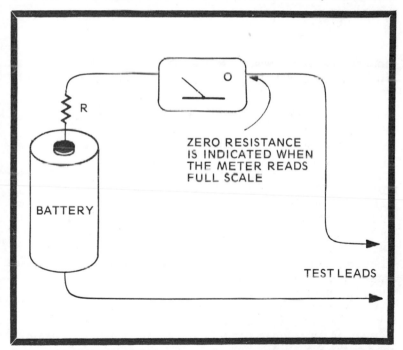

ZERO RESISTANCE IS INDICATED WHEN THE METER READS FULL SCALE

R

BATTERY

TEST LEADS

Fig. 2-1. A simple ohmmeter circuit. When the test leads are touched together, the meter will indicate a current flow. Therefore, any conductor of electricity placed between the test leads will likewise complete the circuit and a current flow will be indicated **if** the conductor is **continuous** (not broken).

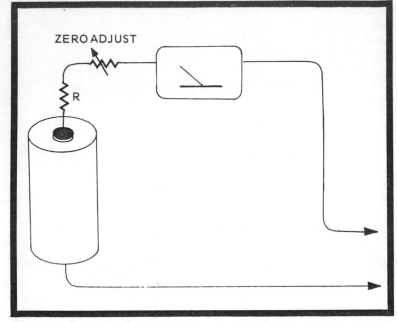

ZERO ADJUST

R

Fig. 2-2. Basic ohmmeter circuit with zero adjust control.

In actual practice an adjustable resistor is used with a fixed resistor so that the meter can be set to zero (full scale) regardless of slight discrepancies in the resistor and meter or when the battery voltage drops slightly. See Fig. 2-2.

The meter can be made to read lower values of resistance more accurately by adding "ranges." For example an ohmmeter with an R X 1 scale might read 50 ohms at center scale (ohms is a unit of resistance and is the amount of resistance to current flow present in a circuit when there is 1 volt across the circuit with 1 ampere of current flowing—in other words, in a circuit operating on 110 volts, if there is 1 ampere of current flow, then the resistance, for direct current, would be 110 ohms), while the same ohmmeter on the R X 10 scale would read 500 ohms at center scale. Obviously, a resistance of a few ohms, such as a motor winding or an element in an electric range, can be much more accurately read on the R X 1 scale than on the R X 10 scale.

In the basic ohmmeter circuit of Fig. 2-2, if the combined resistance of R and the zero-adjust were, say, 1500 ohms, then the center-scale reading of the meter would be 1500 ohms. To make the meter have, say, a 15-ohm center-scale reading, it is necessary to switch in meter "shunts" as shown in Fig. 2-3.

What the shunt does is bypass all but a hundredth part of the current around the meter so that the meter becomes 100 times less sensitive. It will still read zero (full scale) when the leads are touched together because the meter circuit is directly across the battery; however, if there is any resistance between the test leads, most of the current will be shunted around the meter.

VOLT-OHMMETERS

It is not likely that you can purchase an ohmmeter by itself, nor should you want to. Most test meters contain both AC and DC voltmeter as well as ohmmeter functions. A "function" switch on the front of the meter box changes the meter from an ohmmeter to a voltmeter (and oftentimes a direct current ammeter or milliammeter—milliamperes are one-thousandth of an ampere) and back again. This makes it much more convenient to use, since the complete tester necessary for most repair work is contained in one unit. IT SHOULD BE HERE NOTED THAT YOU MUST NOT MEASURE OHMS WHEN THE POWER IS STILL APPLIED

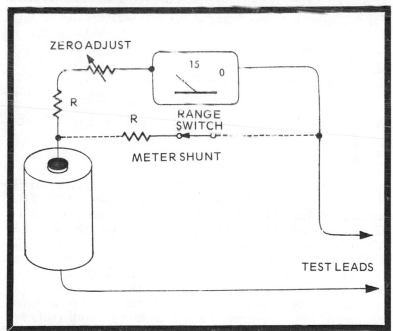

Fig. 2-3. Adding a shunt makes the ohmmeter less sensitive so it will read lower resistances more accurately.

Fig. 2-4. Dial A is the "range" switch which selects the voltage range or changes the meter to read resistance (ohms). There is only one scale on this meter for resistance, with the zero-resistance point all the way to the right and the infinite resistance point at the left (does not move). When the ohmmeter switch is on R X 1, the meter scale is read directly; for example, 50 means 50 ohms, but when the ohmmeter scale is on R X 100, 50 then means 50 X 100 or 5000 ohms. There are two voltage scales on this meter; one is 0-150 and the other 0-300.

TO THE APPLIANCE YOU ARE GOING TO TEST. THE OHMMETER CIRCUIT HAS ITS OWN POWER AND THE CIRCUIT IS MADE TO OPERATE ON LOW VOLTAGE. ANY HIGHER VOLTAGE CONNECTED TO THE OHMMETER TERMINALS WILL ALMOST CERTAINLY DAMAGE THE METER BEYOND PRACTICAL REPAIR.

The voltmeter on an appliance tester, such as the one shown in Fig. 2-4, may read only AC (alternating current) voltage and only on two ranges, such as 150 volts full scale for checking 110-volt AC power lines and 300 volts full scale for checking 220-volt lines. The ohmmeter scales here are R X 1, R X 10, and R X 100, which are suitable for most appliance servicing jobs.

However, VOMs (volt-ohm-milliammeters) such as used by electronics servicemen can be used. These have both AC and DC voltage ranges, five or six ohmmeter ranges, and several milliampere (and sometimes ampere) ranges (for direct current only). The disadvantage of this type meter is that with so many ranges and some for low voltages and low currents, there is more danger of burning out the meter by improper setting of the function switch. A precaution that must be observed with any meter is to always make sure that the function is set correctly before making a test. If you are not sure about the voltage, set the meter on the highest voltage range. Always make sure that power to the appliance is unplugged when using an ohmmeter!

The voltmeter is useful when tracing "live" circuits and to determine if power is present at the input terminals to the appliance. Be particularly cautious, though, any time you are working on an appliance while it's "hot," since you can easily be electrocuted even on 110-volt appliances and especially on 220-volt appliances. Always treat a "hot" circuit with the respect you would a rattlesnake.

The ohmmeter's great advantage is to be able to determine if wiring, switches, heating elements, motor windings, etc. have continuity without having to have power applied to the appliance—in other words, it is the safe way to check for trouble. On occasion, as with any kind of test, you might be mislead by an ohmmeter reading, as for example, you might get continuity in a set of motor windings but the motor will not run. This could be the case for a number of other reasons besides a bad winding, but it could be that the windings are partially shorted; that is, they have less resistance than normal, and even one shorted turn will cause the motor either to not run or, if it does run, to overheat. Since the motor winding may have 50 or 100 turns, one shorted turn will not give a significant difference in the ohmmeter reading. But these are things you learn as you work on appliances and it is the reason why other testers are available for making additional tests. No one tester can be used to find the trouble in every appliance, but the ohmmeter probably will come closest to it.

You can also be mislead in ohmmeter readings if you try to measure everything "in-circuit," that is, without disconnecting one end completely from the circuit. For example, in Fig. 2-5, if you wanted to check the filament in Lamp 2 and you put your ohmmeter leads across as shown, the ohmmeter could read continuity even though L2 is open, since the meter would be reading the continuity of Lamp L1 (assuming L1 was

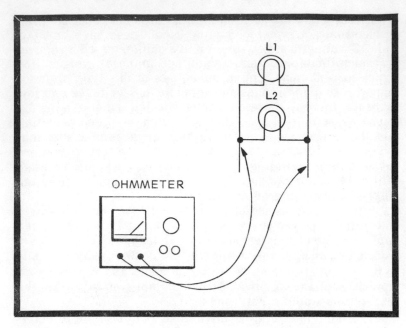

Fig. 2-5. INCORRECT way to check for a defective lamp with an ohmmeter.

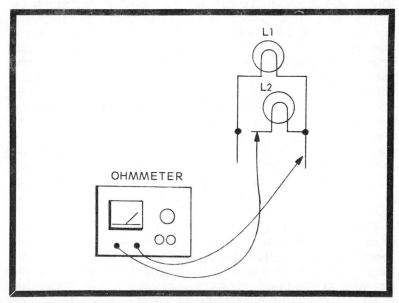

Fig. 2-6. Correct way to check L2. (See Fig. 2-5.)

not burned out also). Fig. 2-6 shows the correct way: disconnect one side of L2 from all other points in the circuit and then measure across L2 to see if it is burned out. (Of course, in this case, it probably would be simpler just to remove the lamp from its socket and measure it.) The point is, make sure when you are reading the continuity of a circuit that there are no alternate routes the ohmmeter current can take to give you a false indication. You can make sure of this by completely disconnecting one end of the suspected circuit.

Fig. 2-7. Zeroing an ohmmeter. Touch the test leads together and position the meter pointer with the OHMS ADJUST knob so that it reads "0" at the right side of the meter. Be sure to set the ohms range switch to the range you intend to use before zeroing the meter. In this case, the meter range switch is set for R X 1, which is the most common setting for appliance servicing (except when checking the shorts between the motor winding and the motor frame or between the element of an electric stove and the frame of the stove; then, you should have the meter at maximum sensitivity, in this case R X 100) Some VOMs will have ohmmeter ranges to R X 10,000 or even R X 100,000.

USING THE OHMMETER

The primary function of an ohmmeter is a continuity tester; that is, to find whether or not a wire is continuous (unbroken). A length of wire even several feet will read almost zero resistance and the actual resistance of a piece of hookup wire is normally not important. If the ohmmeter reads near zero, we assume that the wire is continuous and usable. Before checking with an ohmmeter you should always connect the ohmmeter test leads together and set the ohms-adjust control so that the meter reads zero ohms (Fig. 2-7). Then you are sure the meter is working (doesn't have a broken test lead, a defective internal battery, etc.), and by setting the meter to zero, the resistance readings on the meter scale will be accurate.

The next most important function of the ohmmeter is in determining and comparing the actual resistance of a circuit, for example, in the field coils or windings of a motor. The actual resistance of a motor winding might be, say, 6 ohms. If after zeroing the ohmmeter on the R X 1 scale you find that the motor winding reads, say, 2 ohms, you can be pretty sure that the windings are defective. Of course, if they do not read at all—are open—this almost always means a defect or an incorrect connection.

Unfortunately, there is no actual standard for the resistance of motor windings. For instance, two refrigerator compressor motors may appear to be similar physically, yet the motor winding resistance of one might be 10 ohms while the other is only 5 ohms. But you can compare readings if you have another identical motor which is working normally or if you have previously tested an identical motor and remember the reading. Check its winding and if it measures almost exactly the same as the suspected one, you can probably assume that the suspected motor's winding is probably good, although you can't be absolutely sure since the winding might have only a few shorted turns as suggested earlier.

All "loads" will have some resistance. For example, an electric range element has resistance, perhaps 10 to 35 ohms or so. If you use the R X 1 range, properly zero the ohmmeter, and measure less than 2 ohms, say, you can be pretty sure that the element is defective. Remember, though, that even 35 ohms will look almost like zero resistance on the R X 100 scale.

THE CLIP-ON AMMETER

One of the handiest devices for checking almost any sort of appliance is an AC ammeter. Unfortunately, with a regular

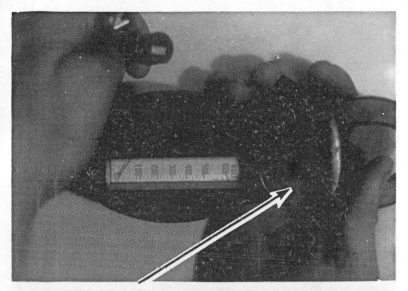

Fig. 2-8. A clip-on ammeter. This particular model has a vertical meter scale and also has a button that can be pushed to "catch" the meter pointer at its highest position. This permits the technician to read currents that occur only for a short interval, such as the maximum starting current of an electric motor. This meter will also do double duty as a voltmeter by connecting test leads to the jacks at the bottom of the meter case. In either case, the meter jaws must be placed around **one** wire; if placed around both wires, there will be no reading or an incorrect one.

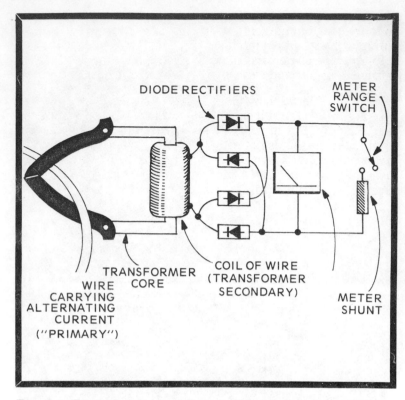

Fig. 2-9. Pictorial view of the electrical circuit in a clip-on ammeter. Wire carrying an alternating current is effectively a one-turn "primary" winding for the secondary winding wound on the transformer core inside the meter housing. The diode rectifiers allow current to pass in only one direction so that the direct current meter can read the proportional alternating current voltage induced into the secondary. One or more shunts can be switched in to bypass some of the rectified current around the meter and so lower its sensitivity. For example, if half the current is shunted around the meter, the meter can be calibrated to read accurately twice as much current.

meter, even if it has an AC amperes function, it is necessary to cut a wire and connect the ammeter in series with the circuit. The clip-on ammeter, however, works without disconnecting any wires and still manages to read the current flowing in the wire. It does it by induction or transformer action. Fig. 2-8 shows a meter of this type. The horseshoe-shaped jaws at the top open and a conductor carrying AC can be placed inside.

The jaws are then closed to form a complete loop around the
conductor so that current flowing in the conductor will induce
a proportional current into the jaws. The jaws are the core of a
step-up transformer and the meter is tied to the secondary of
this transformer and calibrated to read current directly. Fig.
2-9.

Fig. 2-10 shows how the ammeter is used. Normally the
wire is simply placed inside the jaws as in "A" and the meter
read directly. But in case of low-current appliances where a
significant reading is not easy to obtain, you can increase the
meter sensitivity by wrapping one or more turns around the
jaws as shown in "B." One loop doubles the sensitivity, a
second loop would triple it, etc.

MOTOR CAPACITOR CHECKER

Although likely the best check for a defective motor
capacitor is to try a new one of the correct size, this sometimes
is inconvenient, or you may want to verify your diagnosis. Fig.
2-11 is one type of capacitor checker which evaluates the condition of capacitors up to 500 mfd. To use it, connect the

INSULATED LEAD WIRE
CARRYING AC CURRENT
TO APPLIANCE

A ONE-TURN LOOP AROUND
METER JAWS DOUBLES METER
SENSITIVITY. NOW IF METER
READS 3 AMPS, ACTUAL CURRENT
FLOW IS ONLY 1.5 AMPS

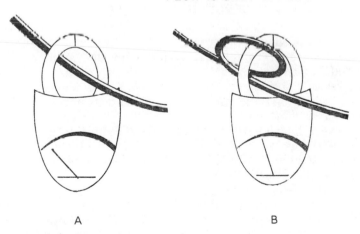

A   B

Fig. 2-10. These drawings show how to use a clip-on ammeter.

FUSE TO PROTECT METER

"ANNIE"

CAPACITOR

ANALYZER

DO NOT PRESS BUTTON
IF LIGHT REMAINS ON

CAPACITY   SHORT   RANGE

PUSH TO TEST

PRESS   TEST   OFF

SELECTS CAPACITY RANGE

INDICATOR LIGHT TELLS
IF CAPACITOR CHARGES UP

Fig. 2-11. Motor capacitor checker.

checker to the suspected capacitor. The lamp should light as the capacitor charges and then go out when the capacitor has reached full charge. Next, you push a button and read the capacity on the meter scale. If the lamp does not light, the capacitor is open. If the lamp comes on but does not go out, the capacitor is shorted.

Be sure to discharge the capacitor by shorting across its leads after this test, otherwise you could get a really unpleasant shock should you touch both leads of the capacitor when disconnecting it from the tester.

An ohmmeter can be used to make a rough check of a capacitor. Connect the ohmmeter leads (R X 10 scale is a good one) across the suspected capacitor. The meter pointer should rise up to zero resistance and then fall back. Reverse the leads and the process should be repeated. If the meter does not move, the capacitor is open. If the meter moves up toward zero and does not fall back, the capacitor is leaky or shorted and must be replaced.

MOTOR START BOX

Fig. 2-12 is one type of manual motor starting box. The leads are connected to the appropriate motor terminals and the box then plugged into a 110- or 220-volt service as required. A light indicates current flow in the circuit if it occurs. If the light does not light, it is likely that the motor winding is defective. Other lights indicate possible short circuits.

There is also a "reverse" position which reverses the connections to the windings. Sometimes it is possible to free a "stuck" motor by trying to get it to rotate in reverse. A motor starting box is not essential to perform the above process but it is a convenience and can result in getting a "stuck" motor on a refrigerator or freezer running again, a condition which perhaps could not be repaired otherwise.

Fig. 2-12. One type of motor starting box. By the means of pushbuttons and lights, this little box will not only help diagnose troubles but may get a "stuck" motor operating again by allowing you to reverse the connections to the windings.

Fig. 2-13. A dry nitrogen tank with regulator valve.

FINDING LEAKS

Every so often a refrigerator or freezer will develop an extremely slow leak, so slow in fact that it is impossible to detect by ordinary means. Yet a few days or weeks after the unit is repaired you can find yourself on a callback with all the refrigerant gone.

When a slow leak is suspected you should apply more than normal pressure to the system. This can be done with a dry nitrogen cylinder and regulator, shown in Fig. 2-13. To use the high-pressure method of checking, connect a hose from the dry nitrogen regulator outlet to the refrigeration system; make sure that all connections are tight. Open the main valve at the tank and set the regulator handle for the desired pressure (say, 250 lbs), then close the main valve and allow this setup to stand for several hours. If there is a leak, even a slow one, the pressure will decrease. To find where the leak actually is, once it has been established that there is a leak, "paint" soap bubbles over all the areas of the system and along all tubing, especially at connections. Leaks will cause the soap bubbles to "puff" out.

You could use dry air pressure for this test, but if the air is not dry you will be adding the sneakiest of all enemies to a refrigeration system—moisture. Dry nitrogen is easily obtained from a refrigeration supply house and can't do damage or cause erratic action of the refrigeration system.

SNIFTER VALVES

Snifter valves (also called Schraeder valves) are often used as service valves. These valves are similar in appearance to the valve used to hold air in an automobile tire or tube. Snifter valves can be welded into the line or they may be welded on a "tee." Sometimes they are installed on "pigtail" lines. Normally, they are not welded into a small suction line because they may cause a restriction. The best way to install a snifter valve is to cut the line, weld in a "tee" joint and then place the valve on the third leg of the tee.

Fig. 2-14 shows a disassembled snifter valve. The body of the valve at "A" is welded into the line; "B" is the valve stem which is threaded into the body of the valve to make the seal. This stem should be removed before the body is welded to the line, otherwise the neoprene valve gasket may be ruined. A cap ("C") acts as a cover when the valve is not in use and keeps out dirt and dust and also helps to seal the valve to prevent any seepage of refrigerant.

To use a snifter valve for testing or charging, the hose you use will have to have a center post inside it to push down the snifter valve stem as you screw the hose on. It is normal for there to be a bit of leakage at the valve as you are removing the hose, but as soon as the hose is off the leakage should stop completely.

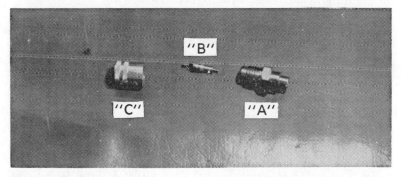

Fig. 2-14. The parts of a "snifter" or "Schraeder" valve. "A" is the valve body. "B" is the valve stem and "C" is the valve cap.

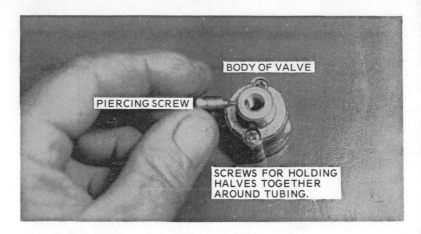

PIERCING SCREW

BODY OF VALVE

**SCREWS FOR HOLDING
HALVES TOGETHER
AROUND TUBING.**

Fig. 2-15. Line-tap or saddle valve shown with the piercing screw removed.

LINE-TAP OR SADDLE VALVES

These valves are installed on the suction lines of refrigerators or freezers to provide a way of checking the refrigerant. They come in all necessary sizes and are ordered to fit the particular tubing size needed; for example, if the suction line is a ⅜-inch tubing, then a ⅜-inch line-tap valve is ordered.

A line-tap valve is installed by placing a firm sealed clamp around the tubing (Fig. 2-15), then a piercing screw (screw with a point on it) is threaded into the clamp to the tubing where it punches a hole through the tubing wall.

First the suction line tubing should be cleaned with sandpaper, then the line tap valve (which is in halves) is fitted around the line and clamped tightly providing a seal all around the tubing on each side of the area where the hole will be punched. The piercing screw is threaded down into the valve by hand, then a valve handle is screwed onto the external threads of the valve. The handle is fastened to a screwdriver bladed shaft which fits the head of the piercing screw. The valve handle is then used to turn the piercing screw through the tubing wall after first attaching a charging hose to the valve outlet on the valve handle. Fig. 2-16A shows a valve handle and line-tap valve and Fig. 2-16B is the assembled valve.

Once the hole has been pierced in the tubing wall, turn the valve handle counterclockwise to allow the refrigerant to flow

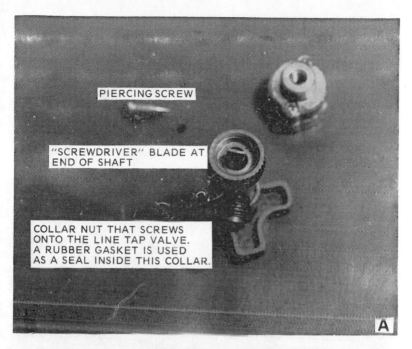

PIERCING SCREW

"SCREWDRIVER" BLADE AT
END OF SHAFT

COLLAR NUT THAT SCREWS
ONTO THE LINE TAP VALVE.
A RUBBER GASKET IS USED
AS A SEAL INSIDE THIS COLLAR.

A

B

Fig. 2-16. A line-tap valve and valve handle (A) and an
assembled valve (B). You should push down as you turn
the valve handle when first piercing the tubing wall.

31

out to the manifold gauges so the pressure can be measured. Once you have checked the system, again turn the valve handle clockwise so the piercing screw will "seat" in the side of the tubing wall and shut off the refrigerant. Remove the handle, also called a "swivel" valve, but the line-tap or saddle valve must remain on the line. Be sure to cap the line-tap valve to prevent seepage around the piercing screw and the tubing wall.

CONNECTING TUBING

There are a number of ways to connect lines together; however, the most common methods used in refrigeration systems are flaring (with screw connections) or swaging. For the flaring connection you use a flaring tool and two "flare" nuts. These flare nuts are a different type than those used for less demanding service such as for water pipes. Refrigeration types are forged nuts and are heavier. To make a "flare" connection, you will also need some type of union and unions come in many styles. If the tubing to be connected together is the same size, the union will be the same size at both ends, but if the pieces of tubing to be connected together are different sizes, the union must match those sizes.

Flaring

To flare a piece of copper tubing you first need to cut the tubing square and straight. You can use a saw or a tubing cutter. Whatever you use make very sure that all cuttings are cleaned away—a tiny cutting can play havoc with a refrigeration system if it lodges in the right spot. Always file or sand away any burrs from the cut end of the tubing and again remember that the inside must be clean.

Fig. 2-17 is a tubing cutter. The knob on the cutter is "backed out" counterclockwise until the wheel and rollers can slip over the tubing, then the knob is turned clockwise to tighten the cutting wheel into the tubing wall. Tighten the cutting wheel firmly, but not too tightly, then rotate the cutter around the tubing while gradually tightening the knob as you turn the cutter so that the wheel keeps taking a deeper and deeper bite, finally cutting the tubing in two.

Caution: Take care not to tighten too fast or with too much pressure or you'll flatten the tubing and make it difficult to get a good flare and seal.

The cutting wheel leaves a burr inside the pipe (a turned-in edge) which must be removed. Most cutters have a triangle

Fig. 2-17. Tubing cutter in use. Turning the knob handle clockwise advances the cutting wheel into the tubing wall as the cutter is rotated around and around the tubing.

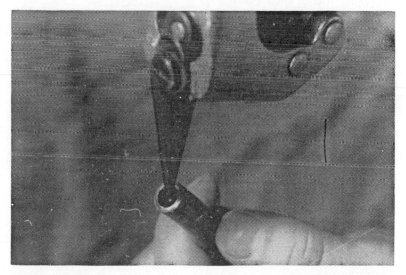

Fig. 2-18. Reamer on the back of the cutter folds out and is used to remove the burr inside the tubing after a cut is made.

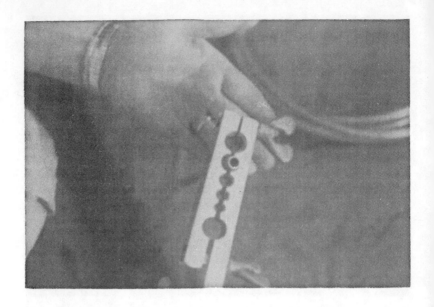

Fig. 2-19. Tubing being inserted in flaring block in the proper manner. **Don't** forget to place the flare nut on the tubing **before** the flare is made—unless it can be slipped on from the opposite end.

blade reamer on the back side for this purpose. You can also use a file. Clean away all residue. Fig. 2-18 shows the reamer ready to be used. The reamer blade turns around out of the way when not in use.

Making The Flare

Place the flare nut on the tubing first. Next install the tubing in the flaring block, Fig. 2-19. The tubing should extend one third the distance of the flare above the flaring block, see Fig. 2-20. Place the spinner handle over the tubing and turn it clockwise into the end of the tubing. Turn the handle about ¾ turn, back it out ¼ turn, then advance it ¾ turn again, etc., until the job is done. A few drops of refrigeration oil placed on the spinner taper will make an easier job and a better flare.

After the flare is made, check it for "hair" cracks or uneveness. If the flare is not "good," cut it off and make a new

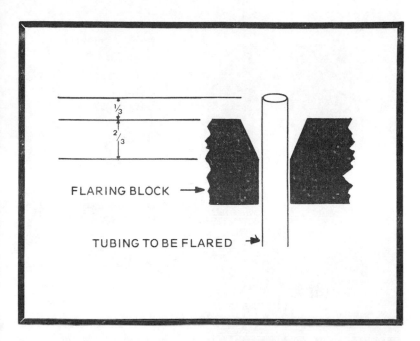

Fig. 2-20. The end of the tubing should extend one third the depth of the flare above the flaring block.

Fig. 2-21. A properly formed flare with the flare nut installed.

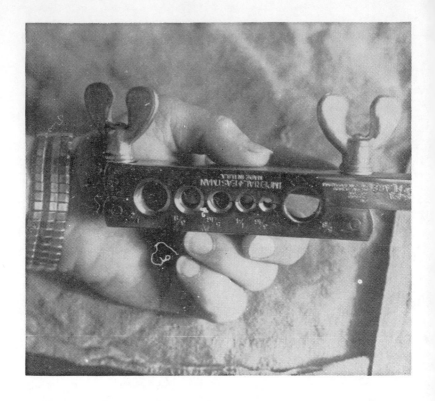

Fig. 2-22. Swaging block with holes to fit various tubing sizes.

one, since the flare will be required to hold pressures of from 100 to 300 pounds and more. Fig. 2-21 shows a good flare with the flare nut properly installed behind the flare.

Swaging

One common way of connecting copper tubing is by swaging (sway ging). This is done by simply driving a special punch into one of the lines to be connected; the punch enlarges that line so that the other end will slip inside it and the two can be welded or silver soldered together.

To swag a connection, the tubing is placed in a swaging block (or a flaring block can be used). The tubing should stick through the block about one inch. Fig. 2-22 shows a swaging block with different size holes to fit various size tubing. Fig. 2-23 shows the block with the wing nut loosened so that the line

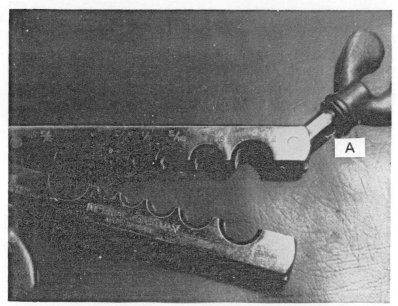

Fig. 2-23. Swaging block with wing nut (A) loosened and the bolt slipped out of the end so that block can be spread apart to accept tubing and so the tubing can be removed after swaging.

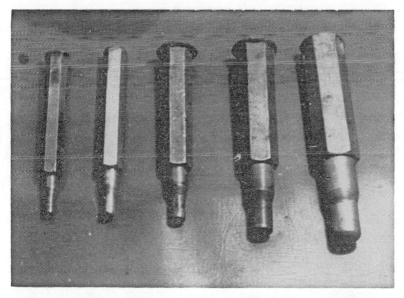

Fig. 2-24. Five different size swaging tools or punches.

Fig. 2-25. A reamer, mounted on a tube cutter, is being used here to remove the ridge inside of the tubing left by the cutter. This ridge must be removed before swaging is attempted.

can be placed inside and removed after swaging. Fig. 2-24 shows five different size swaging tools or punches. After cutting the tubing, a reamer, such as the one normally found on a tube cutter, should be used to remove the ridge inside the tubing before attempting the swaging process, see Fig. 2-25.

When driving in the swaging tool, don't hit it too hard or there will be a tendency to bend the tubing. Hold the swaging block in your hand while driving in the swaging tool so as to provide a bit of "give!" After the tool has been driven into the end of the tubing, you may have to use a wrench to remove it. Do this by turning the tool in **one** direction only (not back and forth) while gently pulling outward as you turn, Fig. 2-26.

After the swaging is complete and the tool removed, roll up a piece of sandpaper and clean the inside of the tubing.

Then apply flux before pushing the lines together for soldering. Fig. 2-27 shows the swaged tubing being checked with the other end of the tubing to see that the fit is okay. Tubing should slide into the swaged unit easily but not be so loose that it can wiggle about. BE SURE THAT THE LINES ARE FREE OF FILINGS OR SANDPAPER PARTICLES BEFORE PUSHING THEM TOGETHER FOR A TEST. TURN THE LINES DOWNWARD AND TAP WITH A SCREWDRIVER HANDLE TO MAKE SURE ALL PARTICLES DROP OUT. ANY FOREIGN MATERIAL THAT GETS INTO THE REFRIGERATION SYSTEM WILL ALMOST SURELY CAUSE TROUBLE WHEN IT STARTS TO MOVE THROUGH THE SYSTEM. DON'T TAKE CHANCES WITH FOREIGN PARTICLES—GET THEM OUT BEFORE THEY HAVE A CHANCE TO LODGE IN THE INNER WORKINGS OF THE SYSTEM!

Fig. 2-26. Swaging tool is removed after being driven into the tubing with light taps of the hammer. To remove the tool, use a wrench and turn the tool in **one** direction only (rather than back and forth), pulling gently outward as you turn, until the tool falls out.

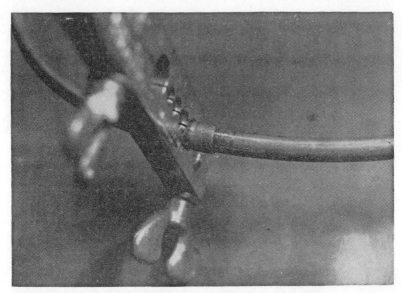

Fig. 2-27. Swaged connection being checked for snug fit. If a joint is too loose, it will take too much solder to fill the space between the two pieces of tubing and the joint will be weak. If the joint is too tight, solder cannot flow in and make a good joint. The swaged tubing should slide together with ease but should not be loose.

Fig. 2-28. "Sweat" fittings can be used to connect two lines together.

You can purchase various sorts of connectors designed for unions, such as tees, elbow, reducers and the like (Fig. 2-28). Always clean these with sandpaper before soldering them in place and use flux if you expect a strong leak-free joint. BE SURE TO REMOVE ANY GREASE FROM THE VICINITY OF ANY CONNECTION TO BE SOLDERED...IF GREASE APPEARS AT THE JOINT DURING THE SOLDERING PROCESS TAKE THE JOINT APART, CLEAN, REFLUX AND THEN RESOLDER.

Chapter 3

Electric Motors

The motors generally used in large appliances are capacitor-start motors, except for the small shaded-pole or split-phase motors used for small loads such as fans. The capacitor-start motor has two sets of windings: a start winding and a run winding. Normally these motors have four poles; that is, four coils or windings wound over the laminated iron stator. One set of windings is called the run winding and the other set, which is offset from the run windings by 90 degrees (¼ turn), is called the start winding. The start winding is wound with smaller wire since it is in the circuit only during the start time—not long enough to overheat.

Fig. 3-1 is a wiring diagram for a capacitor-start induction motor. The centrifugal switch is closed when the motor is at rest, but as soon as the motor approaches full speed, the switch opens and removes the capacitor and the start winding from the circuit.

The capacitor has the effect of producing a lagging voltage field, which gives the rotor considerable starting torque. As a matter of fact, if the start winding, capacitor, or centrifugal switch should open, you will hear only a hum and the rotor will not turn. If the start circuit is disabled and if there is no overload device on the motor, the run winding will soon start to overheat and damage to the motor is likely. Also, if the motor shaft is rotated with a quick spin by hand, it will start running normally and continue to run normally until shut off.

The split-phase motor has two windings the same as the capacitor-start motor; the only difference is that the capacitor is not used. A centrifugal switch opens the start winding when the motor gets up to speed. In fact, you can test a capacitor on a capacitor-start motor by simply shorting it out. If the motor starts (be sure the load on it is small), the capacitor is defective. The split-phase motor will start on its own, but will not start as much load or pull as much load during the start-up time as a capacitor-start motor. Once the motor is up to speed there is no difference in the two motors.

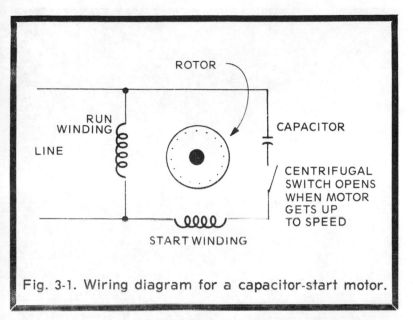

Fig. 3-1. Wiring diagram for a capacitor-start motor.

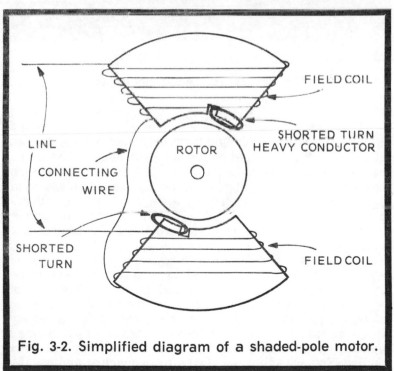

Fig. 3-2. Simplified diagram of a shaded-pole motor.

Fig. 3-3. Electric motor ready for disassembly.

The third type of induction motor is the shaded-pole type which can be used to start light loads only, such as fans. It uses only one winding and does not need a centrifugal switch. The phase lag in a shaded-pole motor results from a shorted turn placed on part of the field pole similar to the method shown in Fig. 3-2. Shaded-pole motors are always rated at fractional horsepowers, where their low efficiency (the amount of electricity drawn compared to the work done) is of little importance.

A centrifugal switch which "throws out" when the motor gets up to speed is not practical on motors that have to be sealed, such as in refrigerators and freezers. This kind of motor is discussed in Chapter 5 on electrical troubles in refrigerators and freezers. The relay-type motor is nearly always a capacitor-start type. Some motors also have a small capacitor permanently connected in series with the start winding. This capacitor is called a run capacitor and usually has a capacity of no more than 2 to 10 mfd, while a start capacitor normally has a capacity value exceeding 100 mfd.

One of the common troubles with capacitor-start motors is the capacitor, and a trouble common to capacitor-start and split-phase motors is a defective centrifugal switch. To replace the switch you must disassemble the motor. Fig. 3-3 shows a motor ready to be disassembled. The dome-like ends are called "bells" or bell housings. There is one on each end of the motor and they hold the shaft bearings. Most motors are held together with four "through bolts" which may have nuts on each end or only on one end.

Before removing a bell housing, it is important to mark the relative position of the housing with the rest of the motor frame. Most motor repairmen do this with a center-punch, placing one or two dots on the bell housing directly across from the same number on the motor frame or housing. See Fig. 3-4. A fairly simple way to mark the bell housing and frame relationship is to place a scratch across the joining areas with a screwdriver or file. If a shaft extends from both ends of the motor, you should also mark the housings so you are sure which is the front and which is the back; that's the reason three dots are punched on one end in Fig. 3-4 and two

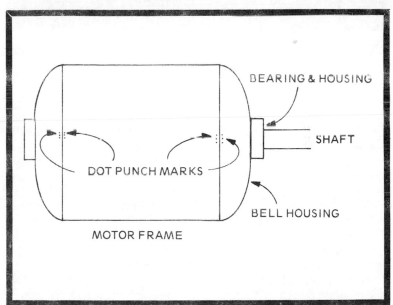

Fig. 3-4. Center-punch marks on adjacent bell housing and motor frame areas indicates the correct relative position of each part.

Fig. 3-5. A cold chisel or screwdriver can be used to pry the bell housing loose from the frame.

dots on the other. (One dot could be used, but it is a bit harder to quickly find a single punched dot during reassembly.)

The bell housing is supposed to fit into the motor frame rather tightly and likely they will have to be forced apart. Use a cold chisel (or screwdriver in an emergency) and drive it down into the seam with a hammer, first on one side and then the other, until the bell housing releases (Fig. 3-5).

When reinstalling the bell housings, line up the previously made marks and use the through bolts to pull the bells into the motor frame securely. A gentle tap with a hammer in the vicinity of the through bolt can make the job easier. If the motor shaft does not turn freely when the motor is reassembled, tap the bell housings with a hammer at various places while checking the motor shaft. Once the shaft turns freely, tighten the through bolts again if needed and make sure the shaft still turns free.

Fig. 3-6. An inside view of the rear bell housing of one electric motor.

Fig. 3-7. A view of a disassembled electric motor showing the stator windings, which include both the start and run windings.

Fig. 3-8. Only the front bell housing has been removed here. The rotor is in the correct position.

Fig. 3-6 is the rear bell housing of one electric motor. The switch contacts are the two half rings at the center. When the motor is stopped, a weighted collar on the rotor shaft allows the shorting ring to connect these two half rings together. As the motor approaches operating speed, the weights sling outward, operating a mechanism which pulls the shorting ring away and opens the start-winding circuit. The half rings are mounted on a fiber terminal board and wire connections are fed underneath to each of the half rings.

Fig. 3-7 is another view of the same motor, showing the stator windings. Both the start and run windings are shown here as they are interwoven in the slots in the stator laminations. Fig. 3-8 is the same motor with the rotor installed and only the front bell housing removed. The fins on the rotor serve as a fan which moves air through the motor windings to keep them cooler.

Fig. 3-9 shows the arms and weights on the rotor shaft which sling out and operate the starter switch when the motor gets almost up to speed, disconnecting the starter capacitor from the start winding, or in the case of a split-phase motor, disconnecting the line from the start winding. Figs. 3-10 and 3-11 show another type starter switch used in fractional horsepower motors.

CHECKING BEARINGS

Most fractional horsepower motors have sleeve bearings which are pressed into the bell housing. If the bearings wear enough to allow the rotor to strike the stator, the motor will not run. The distance between the rotor and stator should be extremely small for best motor efficiency and power, so even

Fig. 3-9. Centrifugal motor switch used in at least one type motor (there are many variations). As the rotor reaches a predetermined speed the weights swing out and move a collar which actuates a switch.

Fig. 3-10. The "spoon" type starter switch shown here is used in some motors.

slight bearing wear can mean a nonrunning motor. Check the bearings by pushing the armature (rotor) shaft into the bell housing while the motor is disassembled and see if there is "play."

If the bearings need to be replaced, get an exact replacement. Drive out the old bearing and drive in the new one, using a shoulder tool so the bearing will not be deformed. The shaft will not go into the new bearing, so you will need to use a reamer to ream out the bearing enough so the shaft will fit snugly—but not too snugly. Use plenty of oil around the bearing and shaft when reassembling the motor. If the shaft is locked you may have to ream one of the bearings a bit more. A trick that can be used is to turn on the motor for a short time, quickly tap the bell housings to see if you can get the bearings to align properly and allow the rotor to start turning. Don't leave a motor that is not turning connected to the power line, especially if there is no overload protector, or the motor windings may burn out.

Another trick to cure a tight motor is to put a pulley on the shaft, lock the motor in some sort of vice or clamp, then connect a much larger motor to it by a V-belt and let the large motor turn the smaller motor for a few minutes to loosen up the bearings. Keep the bearings and shaft well oiled to prevent lockup or bearing "freeze."

Once you can get a motor to pull itself at full speed without load, you can allow the motor to run to "loosen" it up, but be sure to keep a close watch on it and keep it lubricated until the shaft turns reasonably free by hand or does not stop abruptly when the power is turned off.

MOTOR SPEEDS

Motor speeds are determined by the number of magnetic poles or sets of windings forming magnetic poles in the iron

Fig. 3-11. The part indicated in this photo operates the "spoon" switch.

stator. The most common induction motor uses four poles and runs without load at near the "synchronous" speed of 1800 revolutions per minute (RPM). Usually the nameplate indicates a speed of about 1725 to 1750. The latter figures represent the full load speed since induction motors will "slip" a bit when loaded. A 2-pole motor will run at near 3600 revolutions per minute, while a 6-pole motor runs at near 1200 revolutions per minute.

Speed control is difficult with fractional horsepower motors because if the rotor slows down, the starter switch will again close and try to speed up the motor, giving totally unsatisfactory results. Small shaded-pole motors sometimes have multiple windings so that the speed can be changed easily, depending upon external connections which effectively produce more or less electrical poles in the motor stator.

MOTOR TROUBLESHOOTING CHART

Motor hums but will not start

Defective starting capacitor

Starting switch not making contact

Start winding burned open

Spring broken or gone from centrifugal switch activator.

Relay bad

Shaft bearing frozen or severely worn.

"Wear" washer on end of the rotor worn out or gone.

Too high load

Motor runs but shuts off

Too much load on motor

Bearing badly worn or "freezing"

Overload protector defective

Shorted turns in either start or run winding

Motor will not run and does not hum

  No power to motor

  Loose wire

  Motor windings both burned out

  Overload protector open; replace

Chapter 4

Basic Refrigeration Systems

There are only six parts to a simple refrigeration system. Of course, most refrigerators will have more elements than this, but these basic elements are all they have to have.

THE COMPRESSOR

The compressor is used to pump the refrigerant (gas) through the system. The compressor removes the vapor from the low side, which is laden with heat, and compresses it (the vapor or gas), raising the pressure and squeezing the vapor into a smaller area. This raises the temperature of the vapor to above the temperature of the air outside the refrigerator. The heat moves out of the vapor and into the outside air. As the heat leaves the vapor, the vapor turns back to liquid to start another cycle through the refrigerator system.

THE CONDENSER

The heat transfer from the vapor to the outside air occurs in the condenser, which in some units looks something like a radiator on a water-cooled automobile. In these units, there is a considerable amount of tubing folded back and forth through cooling fins. Other refrigeration units use static condensers, or forced air condensers, or possibly a combination of all three. In any case, the vapor enters the condenser at the top and moves down through the condenser tubing where the contact with the outside air cools (removes the heat from) the vapor. By the time the refrigerant reaches the bottom it has returned to a liquid state.

CAPILLARY TUBE

At the bottom of the condenser, the liquid gas flows into the capillary tube which is welded on the condenser output line. The capillary tube is a very small line with a tiny hole through it. Its purpose is to restrict the flow of gas so that the compressor can build up pressure in the condenser for quick removal of the heat.

EVAPORATOR

The cap tube is also a "metering" device that allows the correct amount of liquid gas to flow into the evaporator. The evaporator is inside the refrigerator and is the part of the refrigerator that is cooled. It is composed of a series of coils made of larger tubing than the cap tube. The cap tube meters gas into the input of the evaporator and, since the coils are larger, the pressure is reduced. This reduced pressure causes the refrigerant to "boil," changing it from a liquid into a vapor, and heat is picked up in the process. Because of the suction on the low side of the compressor, the vapor moves on through the evaporator, carrying the heat it has picked up with it, thus completing the cycle.

REFRIGERATION GAS

It is the property of all liquids that they will boil or vaporize at different temperature and pressure levels. Water, for example, boils at 212 degrees F when at sea level pressure. Increase the pressure, and it takes a higher temperature to make the water boil; reduce the pressure and the water will boil at a lower temperature. Refrigerants or refrigeration gases all have the property of boiling or vaporizing at low temperatures, but increasing the pressure of the refrigerant also raises its boiling point. It is this characteristic that makes refrigeration possible. For example, in a refrigerator we want the evaporator to operate at about zero degrees, and for most refrigeration gases now used, this means that the pressure on the evaporator will be about 9 or 10 pounds and at this pressure the refrigerant is boiling or vaporizing.

When any liquid vaporizes, it picks up heat in the process. The heated vapors are drawn away from the evaporator by the suction or low side of the compressor and the heat is carried away. To "wring out" the heat, it is only necessary to increase the pressure so that the boiling point of the refrigerant rises to above room temperature. At this point the vapors turn back into liquid and give up the heat in the air surrounding the condenser.

THERMOSTAT

The thermostat may be considered as part of the refrigeration system since it controls the temperature inside

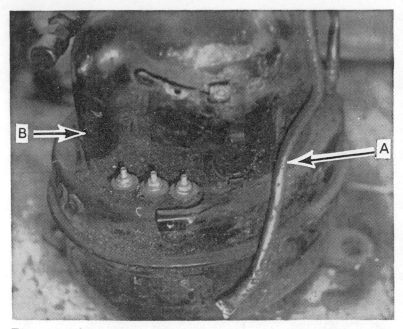

Fig. 4-1. A compressor unit with a service valve (A) welded into the dome of the unit. (B) is the high-side connection from the compressor.

the box. The thermostat (about which more is said later in this chapter) is a device which senses the box temperature and either turns the compressor motor on or off, as necessary, to maintain an even temperature. A knob on the thermostat permits the owner to select the desired degree of cold.

All components in a refrigeration system are welded together in a closed circuit. There can be no leakage in the system, or the refrigerant will quickly be forced into the outside air and the cycle will cease.

THE REFRIGERATION CYCLE

A refrigeration system can be divided into two parts: The low-pressure and the high-pressure side. Servicemen normally refer to these as the "low side" and the "high side." All modern-day compressors used in home-type refrigeration are hermetically sealed, with the motor sealed in a housing with the compressor, which is connected directly to the motor shaft. The compressor, regardless of type, is used to move the refrigerant gas around the system. The motor provides the motive force to the compressor. Fig. 4-1 shows one type hermetically sealed motor-compressor, and Fig. 4-2 is an inside view with the motor-compressor "dome" enclosure removed by grinding.

Motor connections are brought out usually through a glass seal as in Fig. 4-3. Some, however, are simply bolts connected through the dome, insulated by washers to prevent electrical shorts and to prevent the refrigerant gas and lubricating oil inside the dome from escaping (Fig. 4-4). A compressor unit made by another manufacturer is shown in Fig. 4-5. Fig. 4-6 shows an old model refrigerator compressor using an external motor and V-belt drive. Most compressors have a nameplate on the side or bottom that indicates make, model, horsepower, voltage and ampere rating of the unit (Fig. 4-7).

The compressor not only moves the refrigerant through the system but compresses the refrigerant vapor into a smaller area. This raises the pressure of the vapor and increases the "boiling point" temperature. The high-pressure vapor is carried by tubing to the condenser.

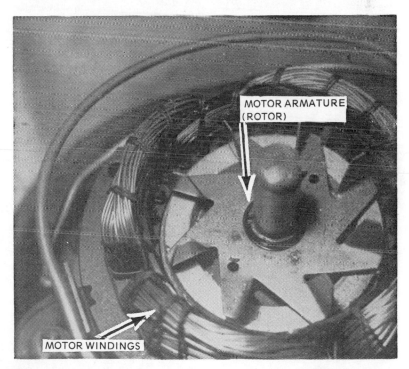

Fig. 4-2. The inside of a compressor unit with the case opened by grinding to show the motor armature and windings.

Fig. 4-3. A compressor with the electrical terminals to the motor set in a glass seal (A). The starting relay and motor overload protector are mounted at (B).

Fig. 4-4. A compressor unit with electrical connections brought out through the side of the case by feedthrough bolts and insulating washers that seal off the gas also.

Fig. 4-5. Another type hermetically sealed compressor-motor. The motor terminals are along the bottom.

Fig. 4-6. An open type compressor with receiver tank (A). The electric motor (on the other side of the compressor) drives the compressor with a V-belt.

Fig. 4-7. A nameplate on the compressor normally shows make, model, horsepower, voltage and amperage drawn. There may also be an indication of the type refrigerant gas used stamped on the compressor at (A).

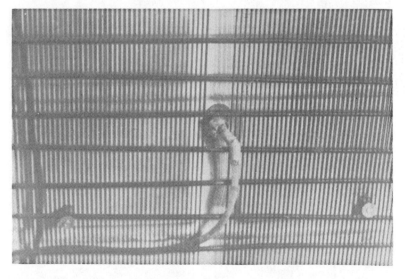

Fig. 4-8. A typical static condenser, usually located on the back of a refrigerator. The "grill" work is steel wire welded to the tubing to help support it and to help carry away some of the heat.

The Condenser

Condensers come in many sizes and shapes. The three general types are the "static" type (Fig. 4-8), the "fin" type (Fig. 4-9) and the "fan" type (Fig. 4-10). Fig. 4-11 shows the condenser strapped or welded to the outside wall of a refrigerator. The hot vapor going into the condenser is cooled (the heat removed) by exposure to the outside air. As the vapor cools, it turns back into a liquid.

So, the basic purpose of the condenser is to remove the heat absorbed from inside the refrigerator or freezer from the refrigerant. Because the vapor has been forced into a smaller area, it becomes hotter than the air around the condenser and

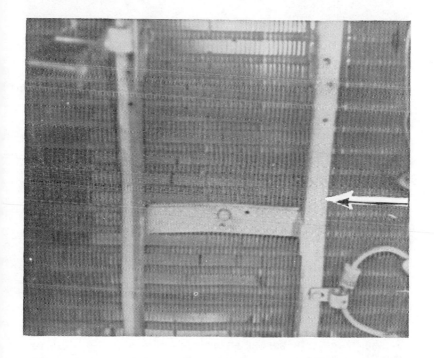

Fig. 4-9. A "fin" type condenser with compressor mounting braces (the H frame at the center). This condenser lays horizontally and the compressor is mounted on top. This is also a "static" type condenser, meaning it relies on natural air movement to carry the heat away from the coils. The fins provide a larger air contact surface to enhance the release of heat.

Fig. 4-10. A fan type condenser is normally used only on older and larger refrigeration systems or freezers. The fan moves air across the condenser, resulting in more efficient condensation in a smaller space.

since heat will always move toward a cooler surface, the heat from the gas vapor is released into the air. As the heat is released, the vapor turns back into a liquid by the time it leaves the lower part of the condenser, and the liquid refrigerant now moves to the capillary tube.

The Capillary Tube

The "cap" tube serves as a restriction in the system or actually a "metering" device that resists the flow of refrigerant and allows only a specific amount to travel to the low side of the system. A drier or strainer is normally connected in the line just before the liquid enters the cap tube to prevent foreign particles from clogging it; the filter also tends to remove any moisture that might be in the liquid.

The size and length of the cap tube are carefully chosen for each particular system, so if a cap tube has to be changed, it should be replaced with one of the same specifications. Both size (diameter) and length determine the cap tube "restriction." Sometimes a replacement may be larger and longer than the original, or it could be smaller and shorter, and still work normally, but be sure that the replacement is recommended by or for the particular system you are working on.

The Evaporator

From the cap tube, the refrigerant goes to the evaporator, the "cold" part of the refrigerator. The refrigerant inside the evaporator is under low pressure, so it will boil off at a much lower temperature. As any liquid boils it picks up or absorbs heat. (It is like putting alcohol on your skin; as the alcohol evaporates, your skin feels cool and is cooled.)

The point where the cap tube empties into the evaporator is where the "low" side of a refrigeration system starts. The

Fig. 4-11. A condenser that is strapped or welded to the inside of the outside wall of a refrigerator. The air moving over the outside of the refrigerator removes the heat. The wall of the refrigerator will get hot when the unit is running.

Fig. 4-12. Evaporator with the coils soldered to the outside.

compressor "draws" the refrigerant through the evaporator, then the heat is drawn off and out of the enclosed box.

The shape of the evaporator is dependent upon its location in the refrigerator or freezer and the size of the box. Fig. 4-12 is an evaporator with the coils soldered to the outside. Fig. 4-13 is a type evaporator used in one model of frost-free refrigerators. Fig. 4-14 is an evaporator typical of those used in an automatic-defrost refrigerator.

The Suction Line

The suction line carries the refrigerant vapor back to the compressor. Usually, the cap tube is soldered to the suction line, for two reasons. First, the cap tube is small and would be easily bent, so the suction line (or low-side line as it is often called) helps support the fragile cap tube. Secondly, and perhaps even more important is the fact that the suction line can act as a heat exchanger. The cap tube heat keeps the suction line from sweating and at the same time the suction line removes some of the heat from the cap tube, thus increasing the efficiency of the refrigeration system. The suction line normally enters the compressor dome at the top and the vapor, which is cooler than the compressor motor, helps to carry away the motor heat also.

More On Compressors

Compressors come in three different types. They are known as low-, medium-, and high-temperature units. The low- and medium-temperature units are usually used in refrigerators that have a freezer storage unit. High-temperature compressors are used for boxes that operate at temperatures above 32 degrees F, such as for flower storage, air conditioners, etc.

Fig. 4-13. A typical evaporator (A) in a frost-clear refrigerator. The fan (B) moves the air over the evaporator. A suction line accumulator (C) stores refrigerant that hasn't boiled off so that raw liquid refrigerant will not be pulled into the compressor.

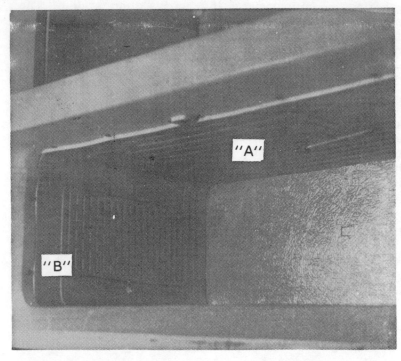

Fig. 4-14. Evaporator of the type used in a typical automatic-defrost refrigerator. The evaporator coils are on the bottom side of the shelf at (A) and also in back of the walls at (B).

The motors in compressors normally cannot be repaired when they go bad, since the cost of service would be prohibitive compared to a complete replacement unit. Compressor motors have two windings, one start winding and one run winding. A starting relay is used to switch in the start winding for a short interval to get the motor rolling and nearly up to full speed, then the relay opens the start winding as explained earlier. The starting relay is mounted outside the motor, usually on the compressor dome, and it can be replaced.

REFRIGERATORS

Over the years, home refrigerators have varied in type and style, but basically they are similar in operation. The older models normally have an evaporator at the top where ice trays are kept behind a door. Usually, there is a "fresh meat" keeper tray under the evaporator. When the refrigerator is defrosted, the meat keeper tray also catches the water as it melts off the evaporator. Defrosting of this type refrigerator is a manual chore; that is, it has to be performed by the owner at regular intervals. Although this is an inconvenience, the food stored inside these boxes has less tendency to dry out than with modern automatic-defrost types. Of course, there are many of these refrigerators still in use.

In older refrigerators with the evaporator at the top, it is necessary to keep an air passage open at the back of the shelves. Air flow can be restricted by placing square dishes against the back wall or by covering the shelves with paper that touches the back walls. If paper on the shelves is used, take care that the air circulation is not restricted near the walls.

The "Spill-Over" System

In some refrigerators there are two evaporators, one for a freezer compartment and the other for the refrigerator itself. After the freezer reaches a cold temperature, the refrigerant "boils off" more slowly, "spilling over" into the refrigerator evaporator, which is sometimes located up and down the back of the refrigerator. In other models the evaporator is along the top part of the box. Since cool air moves down and warm air moves up, there is a continuous circulation inside the box. In refrigerators using the "spill-over" system, a drain pan is located at the bottom of the evaporator. A tube from the drain pan passes the water outside where it will evaporate.

Sometimes this sort of box is called an "automatic defrost" or "cycle defrost." Even though the freezer compartment has to be defrosted by hand, since the air in the refrigerator does not come directly into contact with the evaporator (the freezer compartment is sealed off by a door) not as much frost collects as on earlier types. It does have to be defrosted, but not so often. The evaporator inside the refrigerator part of the box defrosts when the unit is turned off. The frost leaves because the temperature of the box warms up to around 38 degrees, warming the evaporator to above freezing and melting the frost during the "off" part of the refrigeration cycle. When the unit starts again, the frost again collects on the evaporator. The above is the reason for the name "cycle defrost." See Figs. 4-15 and 4-16.

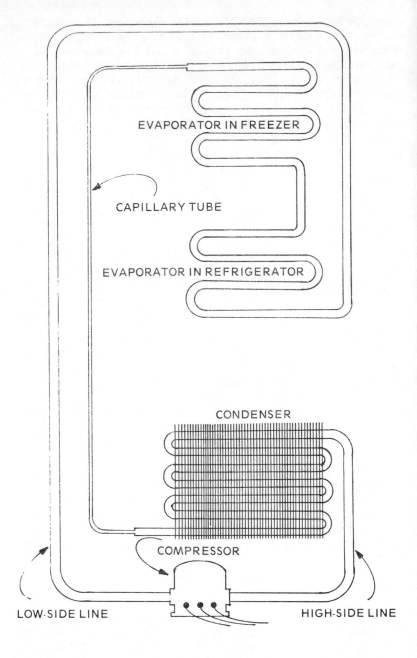

Fig. 4-15. Diagram of a "spill-over" type refrigeration system.

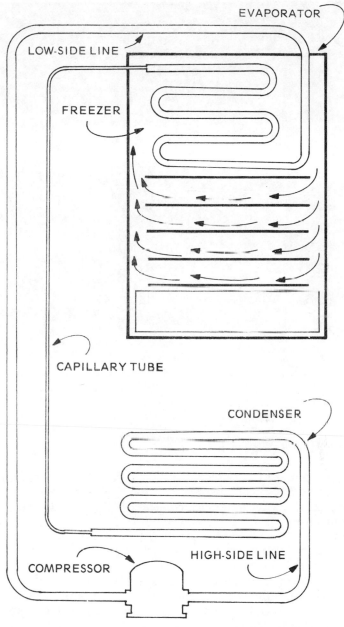

Fig. 4-16. Air "spill-over" system. As the air cools around the freezer, the colder air moves down and cools the rest of the refrigerator.

Fig. 4-17. Evaporator on self-defrost unit. Calrod heater unit (A) imbedded in the evaporator coil and the drain pan (B) to carry the water out.

Frost-Free Refrigerators

The name "frost-clear" or "frost-free" is misleading in one sense. Frost is developed in this kind of refrigerator the same as in any other kind. The difference is that the evaporator coil is defrosted automatically and regularly. Normally, the evaporator is placed behind a panel and the frost forms in this area. Frost forms on the coil, of course, because its temperature is below zero degrees. Defrosting is usually done each 24 hours, using some type of heating system. This may be either a "hot gas" system, or a built-in imbedded heater unit (Fig. 4-17) among the evaporator coils. A special timer turns on the defrost mechanism.

In the "hot gas" system, the timer turns on the compressor unit and also opens a valve in the high side (high pressure side which is also at high temperature) which allows

Fig. 4-18. An enclosed evaporator. Drain trough (A) to catch defrost water. A hose connects from the trough to transfer the water outside to an evaporation pan underneath the refrigerator. A panel (B) must be removed to get to the evaporator for checking or service.

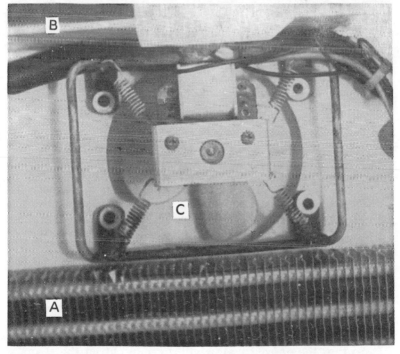

Fig. 4-19. Evaporator in a "frost-free" or "frost-clear" refrigerator. A, evaporator coils and fins; B, ports where air flows out when the panel is in place; C, fan and fan motor that moves air over the evaporator.

Fig. 4-20. Air ducts inside the refrigerator. A, channel or duct coming from the freezing compartment; B, air diffuser which directs air flow evenly inside box.

the hot vapors to flow quickly into the evaporator, melting away the frost accumulation. The resulting water simply drains away. In the "heater" system, the timer turns on the AC power to the "Calrod" heater coil which quickly melts away the ice. Fig. 4-18 shows a drain trough which catches the defrost water. A hose connects from this trough to drain the water underneath the refrigerator.

The "frost-clear" or "frost-free" refrigerator normally has only one evaporator and a fan is used to move the air around inside the box. Fig. 4-19 is an evaporator with the panel removed to show the circulating fan. Fig. 4-20 shows an air duct in the freezing compartment and the diffuser fins which direct the air flow evenly throughout the inside of the refrigerator.

So that the defrost water will not run out on the floor, a drain pan is used at the bottom of the refrigerator in most cases, as in Fig. 4-21. A small strip heater on the drain pan warms the water and makes it evaporate quickly into the

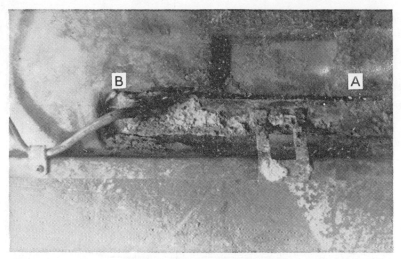

Fig. 4-21. Drain pan underneath refrigerator. A, a strip heater that warms the water to force it to evaporate quickly; B, drain pan which catches the defrost water which flows out through a tube from the evaporator inside the refrigerator.

Fig. 4-22. The arrow is pointing to the drain hose that carries defrost water to the drain pan at the bottom of the refrigerator.

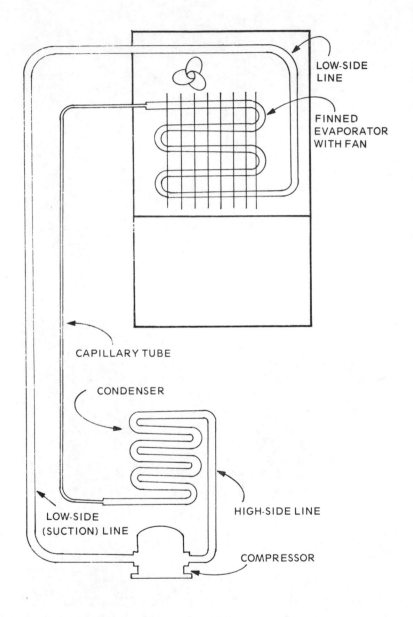

LOW-SIDE
LINE

FINNED
EVAPORATOR
WITH FAN

CAPILLARY TUBE

CONDENSER

HIGH-SIDE LINE

LOW-SIDE
(SUCTION) LINE

COMPRESSOR

Fig. 4-23. Diagram of a typical frost-free refrigeration system.

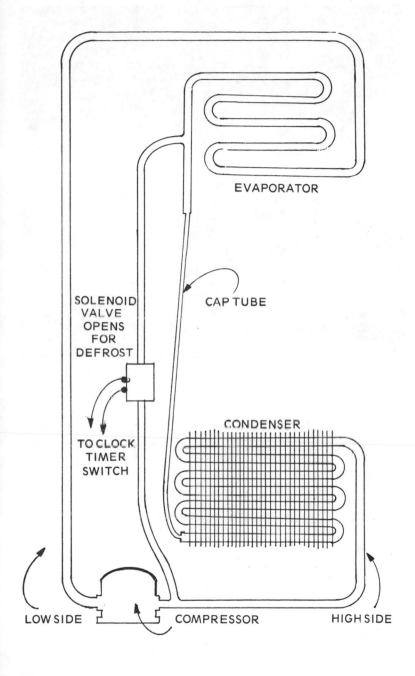

EVAPORATOR

SOLENOID
VALVE
OPENS
FOR
DEFROST

CAP TUBE

TO CLOCK
TIMER
SWITCH

CONDENSER

LOW SIDE

COMPRESSOR

HIGH SIDE

Fig. 4-24. Simplified diagram of a hot gas defrost system.

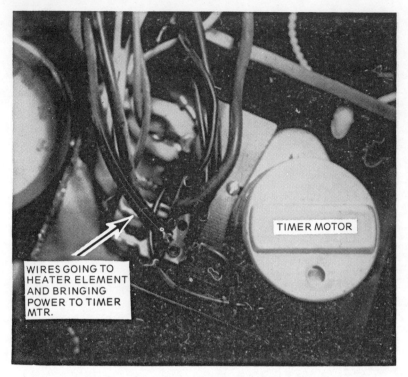

WIRES GOING TO HEATER ELEMENT AND BRINGING POWER TO TIMER MTR.

TIMER MOTOR

Fig. 4-25. Timer motor that controls the defrost cycle.

surrounding air. Fig. 4-22 shows a drain hose coming from the evaporator inside the refrigerator down to the drain pan at the bottom. Fig. 4-23 shows a diagram of a frost-free system and Fig. 4-24 is a simplified diagram of a hot gas defrost system.

The circulating fan on a frost-free or frost-clear refrigerator runs only when the unit is running. The fan also is wired through the door switch so that it stops running when the door is open to prevent blowing the cool air out into the room.

Fig. 4-25 shows a clock motor switch that controls the defrost cycle on a regular basis. The clock motor normally runs all the time whether or not the unit runs. Fig. 4-26 is a wiring diagram of the automatic defrost cycle.

Fig. 4-27 shows the wire which runs from the clock motor switch to the heater. A snap-on ammeter, as described in Chapter 2, could be clipped around this wire to determine if the heating element is drawing current during the defrost cycle.

The heating element imbedded in the evaporator can be removed by pulling it out of the slots made for it in the

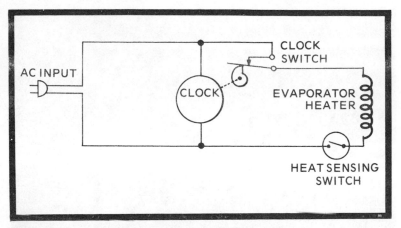

Fig. 4-26. Simplified wiring diagram of the defrosting circuit using an evaporator heater.

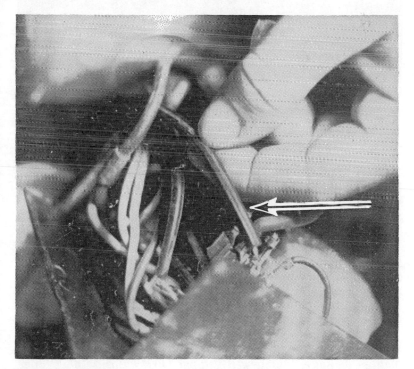

Fig. 4-27. The wire running to the heating element can be checked for current drain if desired by clipping a clamp-on ammeter around the element wire when the defrost cycle is operative.

Fig. 4-28. Electric heating coil shown imbedded in an evaporator. The heating coil can be replaced by removing it from the slots and installing a new one.

evaporator frame and a new one installed (Fig. 4-28). The heating element can be checked with an ohmmeter, as shown in Fig. 4-29, by removing the heater wires from their terminals and measuring the element for continuity. With the leads off, you should also check for a shorted element by checking from one of the element wires to the metal frame of the refrigerator. (Be sure to pick a place on the refrigerator where there is no paint to insulate the ground test lead. The head of a metal screw makes a good test point generally.) There should be no continuity between the heater wires and the refrigerator frame. Any reading on the ohmmeter indicates leakage, which will almost surely upset the proper operation of the defrost cycle.

Also, don't forget the heat-sensing switch that prevents the element from overheating the evaporator. If this switch should go bad, the automatic defrost will not work. If you check the element through this switch, you can assume that both are good if you read continuity.

Checking The Timer

A small window in the back of the clock motor usually lets you see whether it is running or not; however, remember that in some refrigerators the clock motor runs only when the unit is running. Check the wiring diagram. You can test the clock by connecting it directly across 110 volts, but be sure to mark the wires you take off to be sure you get them back in the right places. You can also check the clock motor with the power off by using your ohmmeter (Fig. 4-30). The resistance of the

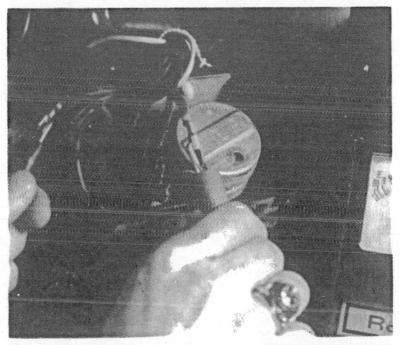

Fig. 4-29. Check the heating element and associated circuit by disconnecting the wires going to it from the clock. The ohmmeter should read about as shown on the R X 1 scale, depending upon the wattage rating of the element. If there is no reading, either the element or the heat-sensing switch is open. Check for a shorted element by connecting one ohmmeter lead to one of the heater wires and the other lead to the refrigerator frame. There should be **no** reading—even on the R X 100 scale.

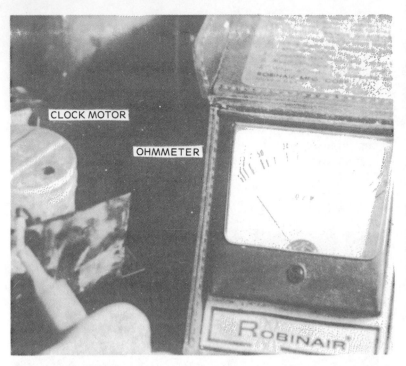

Fig. 4-30. Timer motor can be checked with an ohmmeter (with the power cord unplugged). The timer motor in most refrigerators is connected so that it runs continuously when the refrigerator power cord is plugged in. A few timers, however, operate only when the unit is running. Most timers turn on the automatic defrost each 24 hours, but in some newer models the automatic defrost is turned on for a few minutes up to four times a day. Be sure to use an exact replacement if and when a clock fails.

clock motor is relatively quite high as compared to a compressor motor, for example. This means that the ohmmeter needle may not move much on the R X 1 scale; a better continuity check for the clock motor can be made on the R X 10 or the R X 100 scale. But even if the motor coil checks okay, it is very possible that the motor will not run. The best check, of course, is a dynamic one; be sure the correct voltage is applied to it.

If someone else has been working on the unit, you may find the wires jumbled. Trace them out and if necessary connect them so that the clock motor runs continuously (or as indicated on the diagram) and voltage is applied to the heater element only when the clock switch turns on (Fig. 4-26).

Hot Gas Defrost

Some companies use the "hot" gas defrost rather than electric heaters. The hot gas defrost requires that the compressor be running during the defrost cycle. Basically this system uses a solenoid (electric) operated valve that opens the line from the compressor to the condenser. The hot vapor that normally goes to the condenser is used instead to heat the evaporator coils and melt the frost (Fig. 4-24). As in the electric defrost, a sensing switch is normally used to close the solenoid valve if the evaporator gets to a certain temperature. Some sort of heat is used on the bottom of the evaporator drain pan so that the frost water will not freeze again before getting out of the box.

The defrost cycle for the hot gas type usually lasts only a few minutes, which is why the food in the refrigerator does not thaw out; in addition, the evaporator fan is stopped so that air movement is halted inside the box. As with the electric defrost units, the hot gas type is switched on by a clock motor. Troubles in the hot gas defrost can often be traced to a

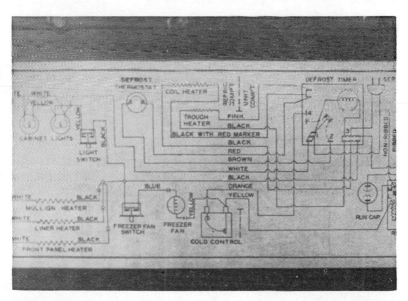

Fig. 4-31. Typical wiring diagram of an electric-defrost refrigeration. Such diagrams are usually found pasted on the back of the box.

Fig. 4-32. Timer on one make frost-free box. To defrost or to set the timer, turn the button clockwise until it clicks. If the unit is running at the time, it will shut off on an electric defrost type; if it's a hot gas type defrost, the timer will start the compressor if it is not running, if it is running it will continue to run during the defrost cycle.

defective clock. Fig. 4-31 shows a typical refrigerator wiring diagram. The timer control of one type frost-free model is shown in Fig. 4-32.

WHERE TROUBLES OCCUR

When a refrigerator stops working, it can be due to any number of reasons, of course. It may be simply that the power plug has accidentally become unplugged, or it may be that a fuse or circuitbreaker has opened in the home electrical circuit. It could be, on some models, that a defrost switch has been accidentally left turned on, or the thermostat turned too far down or off. Simple "cockpit" trouble sources should be checked first, and there are a number of clues and cues to help you out. For example, if the light inside the box turns on when you open the refrigerator door, you know that the AC power is no doubt okay. But some boxes do not have an inside light and in others it may be burned out. Turn up the thermostat and notice if the compressor motor starts or tries to start. If it does you know that the AC power is probably normal; though it could be low, in which case the compressor cannot get up to speed and consequently trips the overload protector within a few seconds. It is essential that the refrigeration serviceman carries an accurate AC voltmeter so that line voltage can be checked to determine if it is within tolerance.

The Thermostat

A thermostat is used to automatically control the temperature inside the box. It is preset for the desired temperature, and afterward should continue to cycle the refrigerator often enough to maintain this preset temperature. When you move the knob on a thermostat to a colder position, spring tension on the thermostatic switch is increased so that

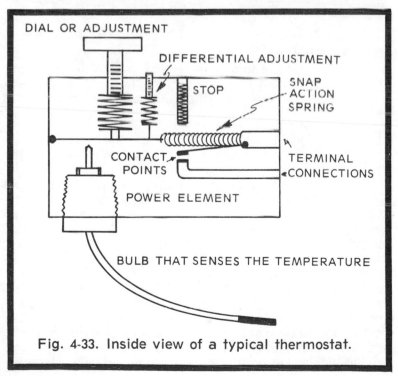

Fig. 4-33. Inside view of a typical thermostat.

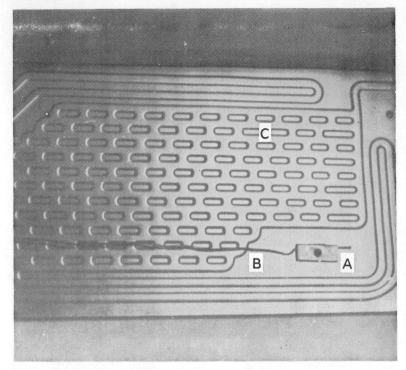

Fig. 4-34. A thermostat bulb is connected to the evaporator at (A). The bulb in this case is held with a bracket and screw. The capillary tube going to the thermostat is shown at (B). (C) is a spill-over type evaporator.

the refrigerator unit runs longer before the temperature is cold enough to force the switch contacts apart and stop the unit.

Thermostats have a small, sealed "capillary" tube filled with some type of refrigerant. The refrigerant inside the tube contracts or expands, pushing on a diaphragm which closes or opens the switch contacts supplying power to the compressor motor. See Fig. 4-33. As the refrigerant cools, there is less pressure inside the capillary tube and the pressure on the diaphragm is reduced. Finally, the switch contacts snap open and disconnect the compressor unit from the AC line. The opposite effect occurs when the temperature inside the refrigerator rises; the pressure inside the cap tube increases and the switch is turned on, starting the compressor unit. The manual preset simply increases or decreases the set tension on the diaphragm or moves the switch contacts closer or farther apart so that the diaphragm has to move less or more before switch action occurs.

The capillary tube may have a "bulb" at the end, but, in any case, part of it is either mounted along side the evaporator walls or it may be stuck inside a tube that is welded to the suction (low-side) line leaving the evaporator. Fig. 4-34 shows installation of the bulb on the evaporator. Obviously, a replacement thermostat must be designed for the refrigerator on which it is to be used.

To replace a thermostat: Remove the dial and usually you will find the thermostat is held in place with two screws. By removing the mounting screws the thermostat can be taken out. (Remember to disconnect the power line before taking out the thermostat, since there are electrical connections made on the back of it.) Usually, there are two terminals on the thermostat, but often you may find one wire on one terminal and two wires on the other. The single wire generally goes to the relay terminal (motor-starting relay on or near the compressor unit). One of the two wires on the other terminal probably goes to the power line and the other to the door light

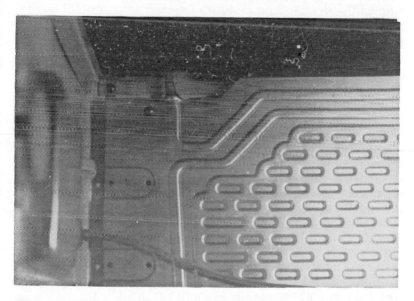

Fig. 4-35. A thermostat is sometimes mounted between the walls of the refrigerator with an external dial. To remove the thermostat, slip off the dial; in some cases the dial screws off or the center portion of the dial unscrews and then the main dial can be removed. After removing the dial, mounting screws or tabs will be visible.

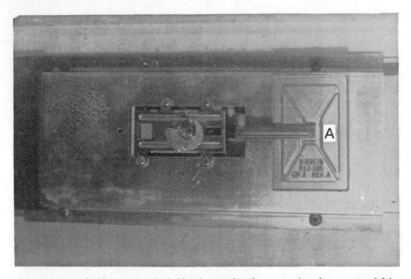

Fig. 4-36. A thermostat that controls an air damper (A). As you turn the knob to a colder position, the thermostat allows the door to open wider. To maintain control of the temperature, the thermostat closes and opens the door to determine the amount of air flow. The air flowing through the door comes from the freezing compartment of the refrigerator. This kind of thermostat is for controlling the box temperature in a frost-clear refrigerator. The freezer unit is controlled by a conventional thermostat.

switch. If the wires are connected incorrectly when a thermostat is replaced you may find that the door light will not turn on except when the compressor is running. It is always a good idea to mark the wires or make yourself a simple wiring diagram and tape it inside the refrigerator, especially if the thermostat has to be ordered and a wait is involved.

Take care when pulling out the thermostat because quite often the capillary tube is coiled up behind it; carelessness may cause a kink in the tube. In some refrigerators, the cap tube runs inside the insulation and comes out a hole further back in the box. If you remove the thermostat, tie a cord to the end of the cap tube so that as you pull out the tube the cord will feed into the hole. It then is a simple matter to replace the cap tube by simply tying it to the cord and pulling it back through the insulation and out the hole. Even with the cord, you sometimes have difficulty—but without it you are sure to have trouble! Some thermostat controls are mounted outside the box as indicated in Fig. 4-35.

Before you remove and replace a thermostat, however, be as sure as you can that the thermostat really is at fault. After pulling out the "stat" so you can see the electrical terminals, short across the two terminals (the refrigerator must be plugged in while the terminals are shorted), and see if the compressor unit starts; if it does (and wouldn't before), the thermostat switch is defective. In some instances, it may be possible to replace the only switch, rather than the entire thermostat, but in most cases it is best to replace the entire unit if feasible.

If the thermostat doesn't control the temperature properly, you must replace it also. But remember, if the refrigeration gas in the system is a little low, the evaporator will not get cold enough in the proper places and the thermostat—even though normal—will not control the temperature correctly and perhaps hardly at all. Fig. 4-36 shows an extra thermostat on a "frost-clear" refrigerator that opens or closes a door controlling the air flow inside the refrigerator.

CHECKING THE REFRIGERANT

To accurately determine just what is going on inside a refrigeration system, gauges are essential. Most repairmen use a pair of gauges mounted on a guage manifold as in Fig. 4-37. The gauge on the left is either a low-pressure gauge or a compound gauge, one that reads both inches of vacuum and moderate amounts of pressure. The gauge on the right is a high-pressure gauge, usually calibrated from zero to 500 pounds. Notice that the left-hand valve, when closed, will still allow the low-pressure gauge to read pressure when its hose is connected to the low side of the refrigeration system. With the center hose connected to a refrigerant drum, opening the left hand valve allows the refrigerant gas to flow through to the low side of the refrigerator system. Obviously, when the valve is open, the left-hand gauge will read the pressure in the refrigerant drum, so it is necessary to shut off the valve in order to read the pressure in the system after allowing gas to flow into the system.

Refrigeration repairmen always try to use only the low-pressure checks whenever possible because there is a greater probability of leaks when working in or installing tap valves in the high-pressure side of the system. "Low side" and "high side" are terms used by refrigeration men to indicate the low-pressure and high-pressure sides of the system as indicated earlier. The intake of a compressor is the low side, while the output is the high side. Pressure on the low side while running

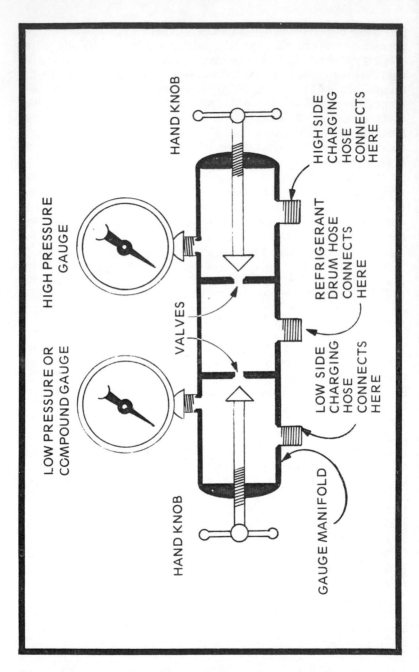

Fig. 4-37. Diagram of a typical gauge manifold and gauges used in checking refrigerators.

probably won't exceed about 10 pounds while the high side pressure may be 200 or more.

It is not unusual to find, when the refrigerator will not get cold enough, that the refrigerant gas is low. To determine if this is the cause, locate the suction line, which is usually the larger of two lines leaving the compressor. Usually, also, there is a capillary tube welded to the outside of the suction (or low-side) line. On some compressors the suction line comes out of the top of the compressor dome, but on other models it doesn't. Some models have service valves as shown in Fig. 4-38. In other cases you will have to install a line-tap valve, which may be located on the "pigtail" coming off the compressor as shown in Fig. 4-39. Or if the refrigerant has leaked out completely for some reason, a snifter valve can be installed by cutting off the pigtail at the "crimped end" area.

Fig. 4-39 shows a swivel valve installed on a line-tap valve. Take care that the valve is placed on the low-side or suction line. At B and C in Fig. 4-39, you see lines going to the condenser on each side of the refrigerator. One side could be used as a refrigerant oil cooler. The refrigerant vapor coming from

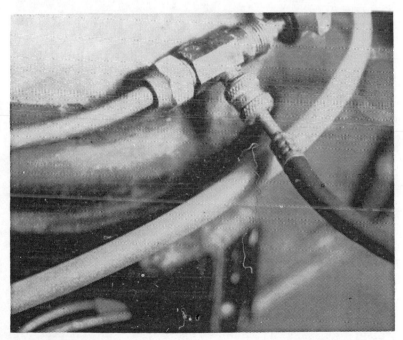

Fig. 4-38. Some refrigerators have a service valve mounted as shown.

Fig. 4-39. A swivel valve installed on the line-tap valve and mounted on the suction or low-side line to the compressor at (A). Take care that the right line (the low side) is tapped and not the high side. Line B is going to the condenser, which is in two parts and mounted on each side of the refrigerator. One side may be used as an oil cooler. In this case the refrigerant vapor coming from the compressor goes up to the top of one side and cools the refrigerant, then passes through the oil sump to cool the oil.

the compressor goes up to the top on one side, cools the refrigerant, then passes through the oil sump, cooling the oil and returning to the other side where the remainder of the vapor is condensed by cooling it. Install the low-side gauge or compound gauge on the suction line. Normally, the high side does not have a service valve, since the pressure is so great that there is always danger of leakage.

Note: If a high-side valve has been installed, always check around it for leaks (as explained elsewhere in this chapter). If a high-side valve must be installed, usually the best way is to install a line-tap valve and then, after the unit has been

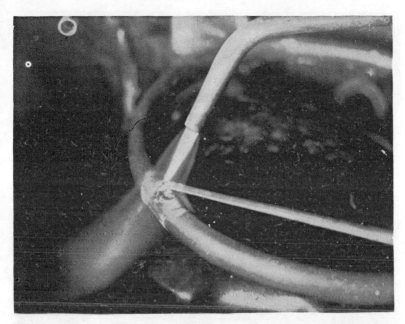

Fig. 4-40. Repairman is welding shut a hole left by a line-tap valve.

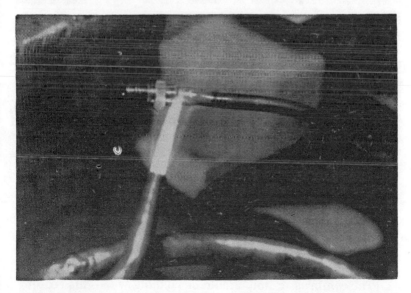

Fig. 4-41. Snifter valve is being welded to the refrigerant tubing instead of using a line-tap valve.

Fig. 4-42. The compound gauge on the left shows that the system has vacuum on the low side.

repaired and before the refrigerant is installed, remove the line-tap valve and install a snifter valve or weld the hole in the tubing shut. Fig. 4-40 shows a repairman closing the hole left by a line-tap valve. Be sure to clean the line and use flux before trying to close the hole. Fig. 4-42 shows a snifter valve being welded onto the pigtail line to replace a line-tap valve so that the system can be easily recharged with refrigerant.

Reading The Gauges

After installing the low-side or compound gauge on the suction line, open the valve on the suction line so that the pressure or vacuum can be read. The hand valve on the gauge manifold should be closed—turned clockwise. Read the pressure or vacuum on the low-side gauge as shown in Fig. 4-42. (The compressor unit should be running when this reading is made.) If the gauge reads down into a vacuum, it could mean that the system is low on refrigerant gas, the capillary tube could be freezing up (because of moisture in the system), or the capillary tube could be clogged, thus preventing the passage of the gas.

Often, if you open the freezer door, you can hear the refrigerant spraying into the evaporator. If you can hear the spray, you know that the capillary tube is open (don't confuse this capillary tube with the capillary tube used on the thermostat; the cap tube we are now discussing is in the system and the refrigerant must circulate through it). If you can determine that the cap tube is passing the refrigerant, you should then connect the center hose from your gauge manifold to a refrigerant drum containing the correct refrigerant for the compressor being serviced. Once the hose is connected, open the service drum valve and bleed the air out of the hose by loosening the hose connection where it connects to the gauge manifold. You are now ready to insert refrigerant (charge) into the system.

If a refrigerator reads a vacuum on the compound gauge, it normally means that it is low on gas (refrigerant). Be sure to allow the refrigerator to run a few minutes before making readings, since a few models may read "in the vacuum" when first started and then rise to normal pressure which is usually about 9 pounds. To charge the system, allow the gas to enter in small "spurts" so as to not overload the compressor. Turn the valve on the compound gauge counterclockwise and allow gas to flow for a few seconds (do not open the valve all the way), then shut the valve and allow the gauge reading to settle. It should move up from its original position, indicating that the capillary tube is okay. You want to make sure about the cap tube, since you can overload the system and burst a line on the high-pressure side.

If the cap tube is open, open the valve on the gauge manifold and allow gas to flow into the system. Close the valve every so often and check the pressure, which should end up at about 9 pounds for most refrigerants. (9 pounds of pressure means the evaporator temperature should run from zero to about -10 degrees F.)

The best way to achieve normal pressure is to stop adding gas when the gauge reads about 5 pounds and allow the unit to run for awhile. Check the temperature in the evaporator. As the temperature decreases, you may find that the pressure gauge will move higher or it may go lower. When the frozen food chest approaches its normal operating temperature, you can either bleed off or add gas as necessary (to bleed off gas, close the valve on the manifold and loosen the hose connection going to the refrigerator for a few seconds).

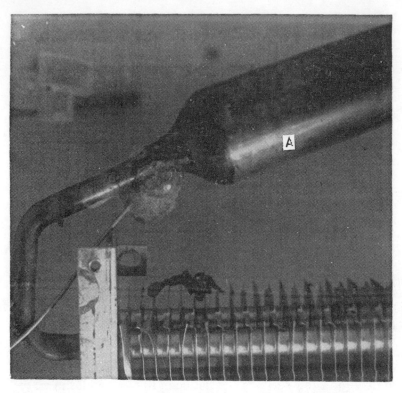

Fig. 4-43. A leak in a seam at the evaporator connection is revealed by soap bubbles. The letter A indicates the suction line accumulator.

If everything is working normally, the evaporator in the refrigerator should start to frost. Next, you should check the system for leaks. This can be done either with a halide torch (the flame changes hue when gas leaks into it) or with soap bubbles. Fig. 4-43 shows a leak in a welded seam at the evaporator, using soap bubbles as an indicator. If a leak is found in the system, you will have to bleed out the gas and repair the leak. After repairing the leak, it is essential to remove all moisture from the system by pulling it down to a vacuum with a vacuum pump. Close the charging cylinder valve, disconnect the hose from the cylinder and attach the same hose to the vacuum pump. Turn on the pump and allow it to run for two or three hours. After evacuation the system can be recharged. Check it once more for leaks. If all is now okay, remove the charging hose after closing the valve on the service drum (cylinder). Close the swivel valve on the suction line and remove the hose.

If The Capillary Tube Freezes Up

Sometimes a refrigerator system will accumulate moisture. This often happens when a system has been opened or if it loses its charge through a leak. A symptom of this trouble is evident when the evaporator freezes for awhile, thaws out, and then freezes again. The reason is that the moisture in the system freezes on the end of the capillary tube and stops the flow of the refrigerant gas. The evaporator then warms up, the ice melts, and the refrigerant starts to flow again until the moisture again freezes.

When the cap tube freezes and the refrigerant flow stops, the low side of the system will read a vacuum on the gauges. When it thaws out, the low-side pressure will rise again to where it should be. Trying to charge a system containing moisture can easily result in an overcharge and the bursting of a line on the high side. When moisture is suspected, bleed off all the refrigerant and use a vacuum pump, as described earlier, to pull the entire system down into a vacuum and draw off all moisture. You should let the vacuum pump on the system for several hours to make sure all the moisture is removed.

To make sure no trace of moisture remains in the system you can install a drier. After the system has been pulled down to a vacuum charge the system with refrigerant to **zero** pressure with the refrigerator unplugged. Install the drier just before the point where the refrigerant goes into the capillary tube. Sweat solder the connections, one end to the capillary tube and the other end to the line from the condenser. **Caution**: If you cut the line to install a drier while the system is down to a vacuum, air will be drawn into the system. Since air contains moisture you will be back where you started. After installing a drier, add some refrigerant to the system and check for leaks. Then bleed off the refrigerant and pull down on a vacuum again for a few hours before recharging. This time start the compressor as you recharge. If a system has a lot of moisture in it, it may take several driers and a long period of evacuation. Since the system operates below 32 degrees F, if there is any moisture at all, it will freeze up and cause trouble.

If The Capillary Tube Is Clogged

It sometimes happens that some loose particles are floating around in a system and eventually they end up in the "cap" tube. When you read the gauges you find a vacuum on the low side, since all the refrigerant has been pumped to the high side. Adding refrigerant simply overcharges the system and can easily cause damage. One way to tell if the cap tube is clogged is to unplug the unit from the power line and see if a vacuum still remains on the low side. Another way to tell is to install a valve on the high side and check the pressure; however, installing a valve on the high side is not a good practice generally, since it is much more subject to leaks than a valve installed on the low side.

If you unplug a unit that has a clogged cap tube, it may not restart because of the high head pressure that has built up. If, however, you unplug the unit and the low-side reading immediately starts moving up and keeps rising until it indicates pressure, this usually indicates the system is low on refrigerant and that the cap tube is open.

If the cap tube is clogged, install a line-tap valve on the high side and bleed off the refrigerant, or you can cut the cap tube off about one inch from where it is welded into the line coming from the condenser or drier. Cut the cap tube with a 3-corner file, notching it on top and bottom and then breaking it to let the refrigerant bleed off. Don't cut a large line to bleed off pressure, since this will allow the refrigerant to rush out and draw the refrigeration oil with it. Be sure to use the correct cap tube for replacement. The size and length are vital for correct operation of the refrigeration unit. You can purchase the correct tube from your nearest refrigeration parts distributor.

After the refrigerant is bled off, remove the break strips or panels so the new cap tube can be mounted along side the suction line. Sometimes the suction line comes to the front of the refrigerator and is located between the walls, or it may be routed up the back. The cap tube, in this case, will have to be removed from the evaporator and a new one installed. To prevent a recurrence of the trouble, install a drier or screen at the point just before that where the refrigerant gas empties into the cap tube.

Capillary tube cleaner tools are available, too. The tool uses oil under pressure to force its way through the tube and clear out the obstruction. Be sure to use only refrigeration oil. To use the tool, loosen the cap tube at the condenser side; you need not remove the other side since the material will end up in the evaporator or oil sump of the compressor where it will do no harm. After cleaning, again it's a good idea to place a screen or drier in the line to prevent sediment from again clogging the cap tube.

CHECKING FOR LEAKS

Leaks are not always easy to locate. A leak may occur anywhere along the line or where two lines are joined together. Often the leak will have a trace of oil around it, oil that moves through the system with the refrigerant and is used for lubricating the compressor. If the condenser is mounted on the inside of the outer wall (between the walls), leaks can be doubly hard to find. The breaker strips and inside shell will have to be removed before the leak can be found. This means removing the evaporator and taking out the inside wall.

If the condenser is on the outside, it is much easier to locate a leak. With the condenser on the outside, you can check inside the box with a halide torch and tell whether the leak is inside (in the evaporator) or on the outside (the condenser).

Fig. 4-44. A cylinder (also called bottle or tank) of dry nitrogen. The pressure on the gauge (A) can be regulated by the valve (B). The other gauge (C) shows the tank pressure and the other valve (D) shuts the tank off.

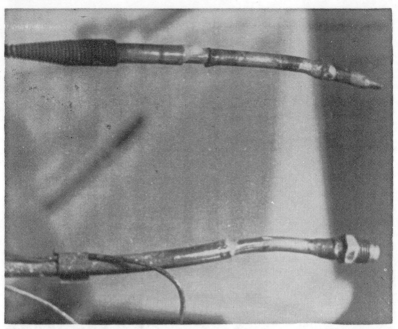

Fig. 4-45. The high-side line (Top) was cut at the capillary tube, a short piece of copper tubing welded on, and the end of this short piece of tubing crimped and welded shut.

However, if the condenser is inside the outer box, it is possible that enough gas will seep in from a leak in the condenser so that there is an indication by the halide torch. Soap bubbles can be used to find a leak, too, as suggested earlier, but unfortunately you must cover all the lines. Wherever there is a leak in the line the soap will bubble out.

To find any leak, of course, there must be pressure in the system. If there is a vacuum present in the system, you can unplug the refrigerator and charge in some refrigerant until pressure is indicated on the gauges. Adding refrigerant and increasing pressure will often make it easier to find a leak. Always give a refrigerator system time to equalize before checking the pressure.

Air may be used as a means of locating leaks, but air without a trace of moisture is hard to come by. The best thing to use is dry nitrogen which is available under pressures suitable for your purpose. Fig. 4-44 shows dry nitrogen in use. The nitrogen bottle or drum should have a regulator valve so you can control the pressure. Pressure can be increased up to 250 pounds, so you should be able to find the leak. You will have to use soap, however, to find the leak bubbles.

You won't always be sure whether or not there is a leak in a system. With the dry nitrogen you can pressurize up to 250 pounds then shut off the tank and allow the system to set for several hours. If the pressure does not drop, you can be sure that there is no leak in the system. Any drop in pressure indicates a leak. Be sure, though, that the pressure has had time to equalize in the system before making the check, since the nitrogen must flow through the capillary tube and this slows it down. Equalization should occur in a few minutes, however.

"Dividing" The System

It is often helpful to be able to tell whether a leak is on the high side or low side of the system, since it eliminates going over the entire system in searching for a hard-to-find leak. The low-side line should be removed from the compressor and a fitting welded onto the end that will fit the charging hose connection. Cut the line also at the junction where the capillary tube connects to the condenser and place a cap on it or weld a short piece of tubing to the cap tube and then crimp the end and weld it shut; see Fig. 4-45.

Fig. 4-46. High-side line leaving the compressor (A), and the low-side line entering (B).

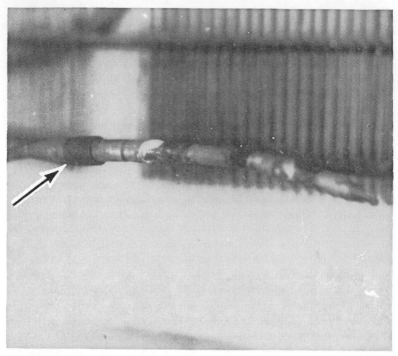

Fig. 4-47. The junction of the condenser and capillary tube is indicated by the arrow.

Fig. 4-46 shows the low- and high-side lines coming into and leaving the compressor. Fig. 4-47 shows the junction of the condenser and capillary tube. This line can be cut, or it may be possible to heat it and pull it apart, as shown in Fig. 4-48. The high-side line should be removed from the compressor and a fitting welded to the line that will fit the hose from the gauge manifold. Disconnect the other end of the line at the capillary tube and weld a short piece of tubing on it, then weld the end of this short piece of tubing shut. The reason for adding the short piece of tubing is so that is is easy to install the tubing back as it was by simply removing the short piece of tubing and welding the two original pieces back together.

Install the gauges on the connections with the charging manifold connected to both the low- and high-side valves. Connect the center hose to the nitrogen cylinder. Slowly turn the regulator valve on the cylinder clockwise to get the pressure you want. The more you turn the regulator valve clockwise the more pressure you will have. When the desired pressure is obtained, check all connections for leaks, then shut off the nitrogen and close the valves on the manifold. Check the gauge readings or mark them so you can tell if they change. Let the system set for several hours, then you can tell whether the high side or the low side has a leak.

This same process works with refrigerant gas, or you can pull both sides down to a vacuum and let them set for several hours, but however it is done, **be sure** that none of the connections you have made are leaky! When checking with a vacuum, make sure that all the refrigerant is removed because a little refrigerant left in the system could change in pressure overnight and give a false indication. If the gauges show no change in vacuum after several hours, you can assume that there are likely no leaks. When checking on a vacuum you should check first one side and then the other unless you have two vacuum gauges on a manifold. (Most repairmen have a compound gauge which reads both pressure and vacuum and a high-pressure gauge which reads only

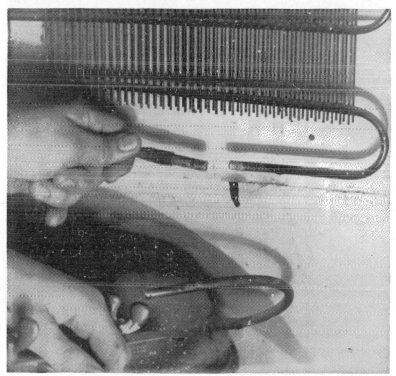

Fig. 4-48. Here, the line has been taken apart between the condenser and the capillary tube. Notice that the cut is made on the large part of the tubing coming from the condenser and not in the small cap tube.

Fig. 4-49. Gauges reading equal pressure on each side of the system, indicating equalization. The pointers are at different relative positions on the dial since one gauge (left side) reads 225 pounds near the top end while the right side gauge reads 225 pounds near the center of the scale.

pressure.) When checking with a refrigerant instead of nitrogen, there is a strong possibility of a false indication, since a change in room temperature can cause a change of pressures inside the system, making it appear to be a leak when one may not exist.

Fig. 4-49 shows gauges reading pressure on both sides of the system. Since both gauges are reading 225 pounds, the system has equalized. Notice that these are different type gauges so that 225 pounds is near the top end of the compound (left) gauge while the pointer on the high pressure (right) gauge is about half way up. The high pressure gauge reads 500 pounds full scale while the compound gauge reads only 250 pounds full scale.

Some refrigerators and freezers have oil cooling lines which go through the compressor, as shown in the diagram in Fig. 4-50. If this line should develop a leak, it is possible to connect the two lines to the oil cooling coil together so that the cooling coil is bypassed. Be sure to cap off the lines coming out of the compressor also.

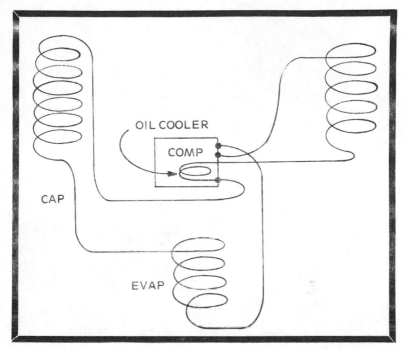

Fig. 4-50. An oil cooling line may loop through the compressor.

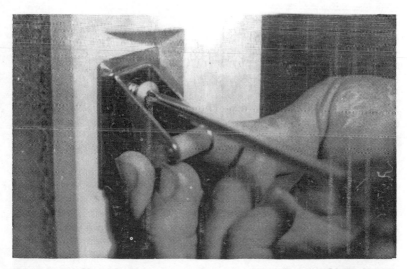

Fig. 4-51. Repairman removing a door latch. Shims are usually found behind a latch to provide adjustment.

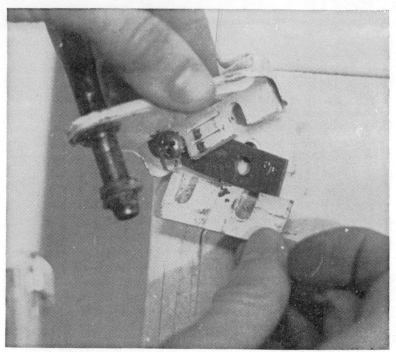

Fig. 4-52. A door hinge being removed. Generally, doors can be removed by simply lifting them off the hinge pegs. Notice the adjustment shims behind the hinge.

REMOVING BREAKER STRIPS

"Breaker" strips are used to enclose the "working" parts of a refrigerator and serve as trim or decorative effects. These strips may be removed when service is necessary. They are held in place in several different ways. Usually, the inside will snap out—that is, the side next to the inside of the box. On some models the strips slip out from the outside toward the inside. Usually, the short side panels will have to be slipped out first, then the other breaker strips will snap out.

In Fig. 4-51, the door latch has to be removed before the breaker strip can be removed. The door hinges may also have to be removed, as in Fig. 4-52. Remove the top door hinge first, then remove the middle hinge. Normally, hinges have a spacer washer(s) between the hinge and the box so the door can be adjusted to make it fit properly. If there is a light or a butter keeper on the door, there will be a wire leading from the box to this unit. In some cases the wire can be unplugged, or sometimes you have to remove a rubber plug so you can get to

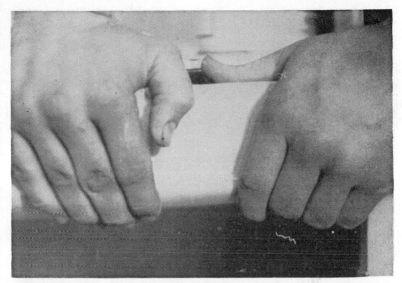

Fig. 4-53. The repairman is removing a snap-on breaker strip. If the strip is in one piece, as here, it should be snapped loose at the center first, then carefully bowed to the strip at the corner.

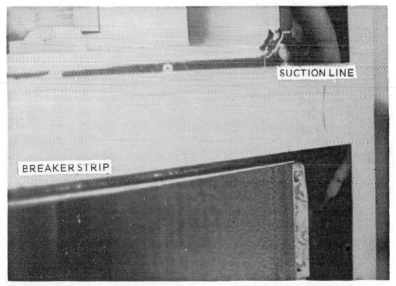

Fig. 4-54. The suction line can be seen here, running between the walls. Still more of the line is covered by the breaker strip.

Fig. 4-55. Screws hold this strip (A) in place. In this case, screws are located on both top and bottom.

the wires to disconnect them. Normally, a door simply lifts off the hinge pegs. Be careful not to lose the bushing which serves as a bearing for the door to swing on.

Fig. 4-53 shows a repairman removing a breaker strip by placing his hands on the strip and pulling outward, with pressure applied by the fingers as shown. Hold the corner of the strip to keep it from breaking. If the top breaker strip is all in one piece, as shown in Fig. 4-53, the strip should be loosened first at the center so you can bow the strip and release it from the corners. Take care when bending these strips, since they are made of plastic and can snap in two easily, especially if cold.

In Fig. 4-54 you can see the refrigerator suction line which runs between the inside and outside wall of the box. In other models the suction line may run up the rear of the box. To remove the suction line, you have to remove the strip marked (A) which may be held in place with several screws, Fig. 4-55. Fig. 4-56 shows a heater that is fastened behind or onto the front strip to prevent sweating or frost buildup. Remember that even after removing all the screws from a particular

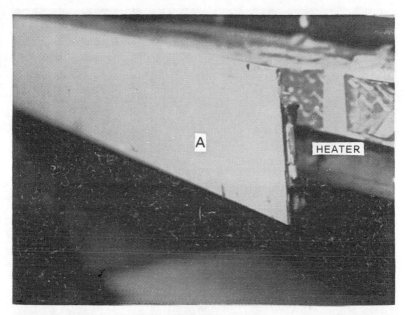

Fig. 4-56. A heater behind this strip prevents frost accumulation. In some refrigerators the heater is taped to the back side of the strip.

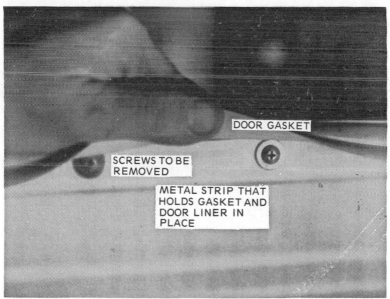

Fig. 4-57. Mounting screws are concealed by the gasket itself in this refrigerator.

Fig. 4-58. Upper door hinge with decorative cap removed. This hinge has corrugations which allow it to move in or out when the screws are loosened.

breaker strip, you may have to slide it one way or the other before it will release.

REPLACING REFRIGERATOR DOOR GASKETS

There are almost as many ways to hold door gaskets and liners in place as there are manufacturers. They use spring clips or screws, or a combination, but usually a little ingenuity is all that is necessary to remove and replace a door gasket. The screws or clips are usually hidden by the gasket itself so that it must be rolled out or lifted to reveal them (Fig. 4-57).

The best way to replace a door gasket is to remove the door from the refrigerator so you can place it on a flat surface. Purchase a new gasket from a local refrigerator distributor or a dealer. Try to get an exact replacement, since it will install much easier and often much neater. But sometimes it isn't possible to get an exact replacement, in which case the only alternative is to buy a rubber gasket of the general type and cut if to fit. Remember that some door gaskets have magnets inside to hold the door shut. For such boxes you will need to purchase an exact replacement if at all possible. If the refrigerator has two doors, the gaskets can be bought separately.

After a gasket begins to crack or split, it has lost its effectiveness and will allow warm air to get inside the box and cause excessive frost to build up, or, if it's a frost free unit, cause the unit to run considerably more and increase the cost of operation. To tell if a gasket is sealing okay, take a dollar bill and close the door on it, if you can slide the bill up and down, the door gasket is not sealing tightly enough. And when you attempt to pull the bill out, it should have some drag on it.

The door gasket should fit the same way all around. Both the hinges and the door latch are normally shimmed to give some adjustment, but if the gasket has lost its resilience, be sure to replace it rather than attempt to adjust the door for a tighter fit. Sometimes the hinges are made with built-in adjustments. Fig. 4-58 shows a hinge with corrugations that provide adjustment. A decorative cap, which can be pried off,

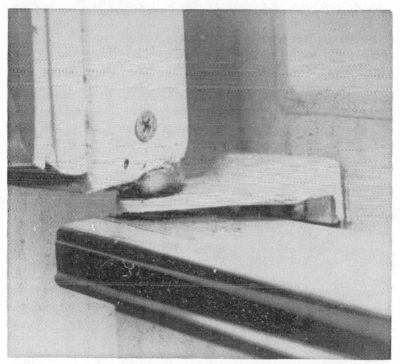

Fig. 4-59. A "middle" door hinge functions as the bottom hinge for the upper freezer compartment door and the top hinge for the lower door. Usually, shims must be added or removed to adjust the middle hinge. The shims fit between the hinge and the frame of the refrigerator, of course.

Fig. 4-60. On this hinge, the screws (A) can be loosened to align the door when a new gasket is installed.

Fig. 4-61. Screws that hold this center door hinge can be loosened and cardboard or paper shims placed behind it for adjustment.

is often used to conceal the "working" parts of the hinge. The middle door hinge, which acts as a bottom hinge for the top door and a top hinge for the bottom door normally is adjusted by removing or adding shims; Fig. 4-59. Fig. 4-60 shows another type of adjustable door hinge. To shim a hinge, as in Fig. 4-61 you can use light card stock or heavy paper.

REPLACING FREEZER DOOR GASKETS

When a freezer door gasket is defective, be sure to get the model number of the freezer. The model number is normally found on a metal tag attached somewhere on the frame of the freezer or it may be stamped on the back of the freezer with block letters. If the information is not available for some reason, take a razor blade or very sharp knife and cut a cross section out of the gasket—be sure to get a part of the gasket that is behind the inside liner or metal strip—and take the

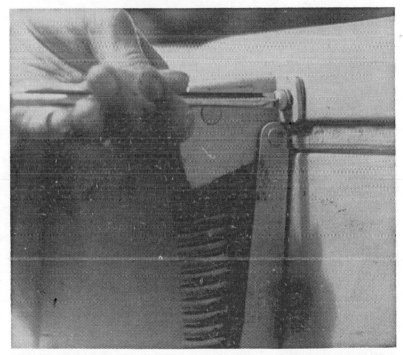

Fig. 4-62. To remove a chest-type freezer door, loosen the hinge mounting screws, but do not completely remove the screws until the hinge spring tension is released by either raising the door or loosening the nut that sets the spring tension.

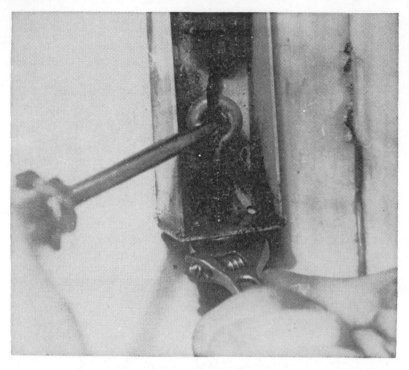

Fig. 4-63. Hinge spring tension can also be released by loosening the nut on the ratchet bolt of the hinge. Be sure to mark the position of the nut so it can be retightened to the same spot after reinstalling the door.

cross section to a distributor for a universal replacement. When making a replacement with a universal gasket, you will have to make careful cuts at the corners and then glue the corners together with rubber cement.

As with refrigerators, it is usually best to remove the door of the freezer before attempting to install a gasket. Any electrical connections in the door will have to be disconnected. Sometimes these connections plug in; other times a rubber plug may have to be removed from the door so the connections can be taken apart.

To remove the door, loosen the screws that hold the hinges (if the freezer has a horizontal door) but do not remove the screws yet because of the spring tension on the hinges that counterbalance the door so it is easy to open (Fig. 4-62). To release the spring, lift the door all the way up past its normal travel, then finish removing the door screws. In many cases, the spring tension can be released by loosening the spring

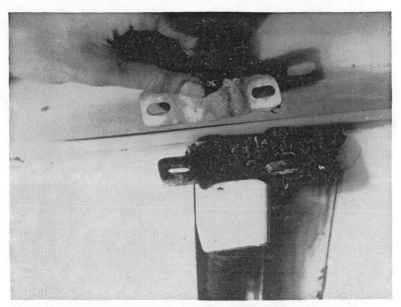

Fig. 4-64. A bushing or shim is usually found beneath the hinge.

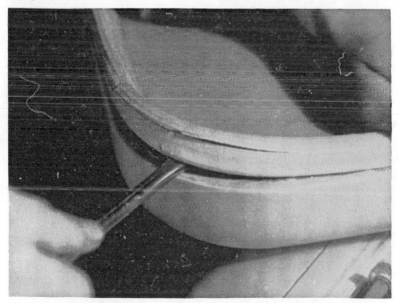

Fig. 4-65. If the liner and gasket are held by spring clips, you should be able to pry up gently on the inner liner to snap out the clips. Continue prying around the door until all the spring clips are loosened.

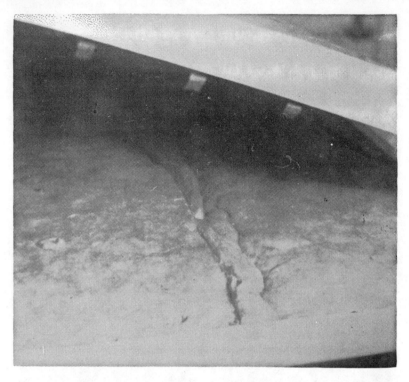

Fig. 4-66. After fasteners are removed, the liner can be lifted away from the door as shown and the gasket removed from around the edge of the liner.

tension nut as shown in Fig. 4-63. There is normally a shim between the hinge and the door (Fig. 4-64). With the door removed, turn it upside down on top of the freezer to replace the gasket as in Fig. 4-65. After the gasket screws have been taken out, the door liner can be lifted out as in Fig. 4-66 and the gasket removed from the liner.

Fig. 4-67 shows the spring clips that are used on many freezers to hold the liner and gasket in place. Be careful not to break the plastic inner liner while removing or replacing the screws or clips. Sometimes the screw holes in the inner liner break out over the head of the screw, so that the screws can no longer hold it solid. You can often satisfactorily solve this problem by using small metal washers under the screw heads to again grip the liner. Of course, the washers must not be so large that they interfere with the gasket or the door closing. Fig. 4-68 shows a gasket being installed on an inner liner. The

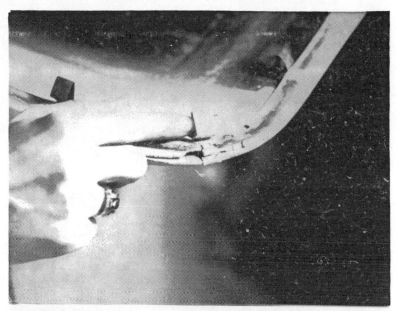

Fig. 4-67. Spring clips hold this freezer door gasket and liner in place. Take care, when removing or replacing them, not to break the plastic inner liner edge.

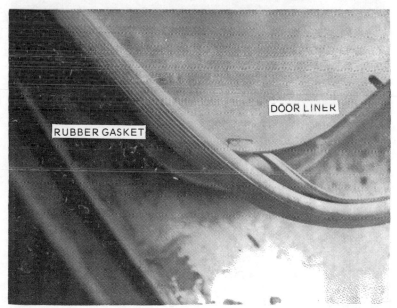

Fig. 4-68. A repairman is installing a rubber gasket on a freezer door liner.

Fig. 4-69. This is how a corner should look after the gasket has been cut and fitted. If the corner is not cut, the gasket will buckle and fail to seal properly. Corners can be glued after the gasket has been fitted into place.

gasket has to be cut at the corners so it will fit snuggly and neatly, as in Fig. 4-69.

When reinstalling the door, be sure to insert the spacers between the doors and the hinges. If the door does not fit exactly, add or remove spacers to achieve alignment. If the spring tension on the hinge was loosened, retighten so that the door will rise slowly when unlatched.

DOOR LATCHES

Many older refrigerators have spring-loaded door latches so that when the door is pushed gently shut, the spring-loaded latch trips and "grabs" the door shut (Fig. 4-70). Sometimes this latch trips closed with the door open and consequently has to be pryed back into the open position before the door can be closed. Do not try to pry the latch out with your fingers or

Fig. 4-70. A spring-loaded door latch.

Fig. 4-71. This mechanical latch is adjustable.

Fig. 4-72. Loosening screws (A) and (B) allows the door latch to be moved up or down for proper adjustment of door closings. (C) is the catch over which the door handle roller locks when the door is closed.

Fig. 4-73. The arrow points to the roller on the freezer door that latches to the hook in Fig. 4-72.

you'll probably end up with bruised fingers; instead, use a screwdriver, wrench or some other sort of pry. If the spring breaks in this type of latch, the front door edge liner has to be removed so the spring can be replaced.

When the door has a mechanical latch, it is nearly always adjustable so the door can be made to fit properly (Fig. 4-71). Often the latch screws have to be loosened considerably before the latch will move because of the corrugations or notches between the movable part of the latch and its backing plate.

Most modern refrigerators use a magnetic catch with the magnets located in the door gasket. If the gasket is replaced, it must contain the necessary magnetic feature.

Most freezer door latches also have some method of adjustment—either screws or by placing shims under the mounting screws. Fig. 4-72 shows a type of latch that can be moved up and down. A roller on the handle is often used to hook over the latch. The roller drops into a slight indentation so the latch will stay locked, but it is easy to unlatch because of the rolling action. Fig. 4-73 is a roller-type handle.

Chapter 5

Electrical Troubles in
Refrigerators & Freezers

One of the most frequent complaints is a refrigerator or freezer that won't run. The first, and perhaps most obvious, check is to make sure that the line cord is plugged in. A good policy is to unplug and plug the line cord back in to make sure there is a good connection; sometimes a plug that appears to be seated correctly in the receptacle may not be making connection. If the unit still does not start, check the receptacle with a voltmeter or test lamp to make sure there is 110 volts (approximately) at the terminals, or plug in any known working appliance to make sure the receptacle is "hot." If there is no power at the receptacle, check the fuse or breaker box in the house. If the fuse is blown, replace it with the same type (assuming that the fuse is the same as called for originally) or with a "slow-blow" type. If a slow-blow type is substituted for a conventional fuse, the ampere rating should be lower, since a slow-blow type will take short overloads, such as when the motor first starts, without blowing but will blow quickly if an overload occurs for more than a few seconds. For example, an 8 ampere slow-blow fuse might be used to replace a 20 amp regular fuse if the only load is the refrigerator plus some intermittent other loads such as a radio, lamp, etc.

Circuitbreakers by their nature are slow blow devices because they are sensitive to an increase in heat caused when the current flow exceeds the rating. To reset most breakers, they must be turned fully off and then turned on. (Some breakers trip all the way to off when an overload occurs; others trip further toward the on position.) Some breaker boxes have fused mains; if one main fuse blows, the other half of the electric service is still live—half the circuits in the home will work, the other half will be dead. Of course, all 220-volt appliances will not work.

Another quick check for power connection is the light inside the refrigerator; if it comes on, obviously there is power at the line receptacle. If the light lights but the unit does not operate, you will have to move the refrigerator away from the wall to gain access to the compressor unit. (On some earlier model refrigerators there is a drawer at the bottom front of the refrigerator that can be removed, allowing the compressor unit to be serviced from the front.)

Some freezers can be serviced through a door or panel at one end of the freezer; others have a grill at the front that can be removed to permit access to the compressor unit. In any case, take care not to bend or kink the copper lines while getting into or working on the unit. Usually, the lines are coiled so you can pull the unit outward for service, but be sure that no sharp bends or kinks occur. Other freezers have to be serviced from the back, making it necessary to pull them out from the wall.

Some compressors are powered from an electrical junction box mounted nearby on the refrigerator or freezer frame; in this case, you can unplug the unit and plug it into an extension cord. If the unit operates on external power, the trouble is either a bad thermostat, cord, plug or wiring. For further tests, plug a 110-volt test lamp into the junction box, then plug in the refrigerator or freezer cord. If the light does not light, try placing a jumper wire across the thermostat terminals; if the lamp now lights, install a new thermostat. If not, check the wiring. Unplug the power line cord, take off the junction box cover and check the wiring with an ohmmeter or

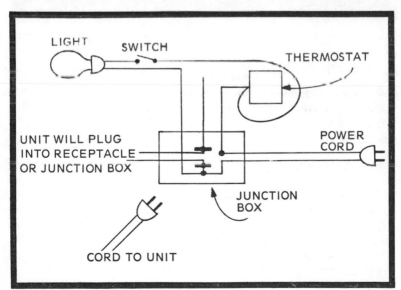

Fig. 5-1. Diagram of the wiring in a typical refrigerator or freezer junction box.

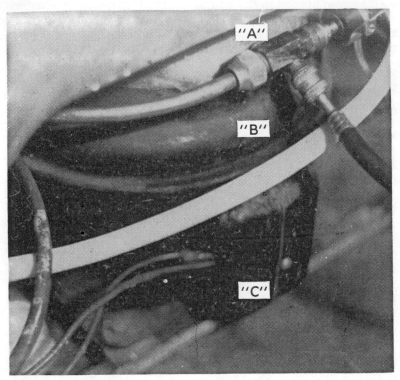

Fig. 5-2. View of a typical freezer unit. Visible are the service valve (A), the compressor (B) and the cover concealing the relay and motor terminals.

test lamp. (Some junction boxes are riveted together; therefore, the rivets have to be drilled out in order to get inside the box. Fig. 5-1 shows how wiring is normally connected inside a junction box.

UNIT DOESN'T RUN

If the unit does not run when connected directly to the power line, you know that there is trouble somewhere in the unit itself. Sometimes the unit will try to start but won't. In this case you may hear a hum for a few seconds when the unit is first plugged in. The hum stops because an automatic overload switch opens. In a few seconds you will hear a click as the overload switch turns on again and the hum sequence is repeated.

If you hear no hum or click, you may suspect that the overload relay or switch is defective. Usually, the overload has a cover that can be removed either by removing screws or a spring clip (Fig. 5-2 shows an overload relay with a cover held on by one screw; the cover also encloses the motor terminals.) After disconnecting the power line (unplug from the wall receptacle), remove the overload cover so you can make the necessary checks. Look for a defective overload relay or broken wire if the unit will not try to start. If it is trying to start, the trouble may be a defective motor-starting capacitor, a burned-out winding in the motor, or the compressor could be locked.

The capacitor is normally mounted on the side of the terminal box near the compressor and should be checked first when the unit is trying to start. You can use a capacitor checker or you can simply temporarily connect a known good capacitor of near the same or the same electrical value.

An ohmmeter can also give you a relative indication of the capacitor's condition; however, you can be deceived. To check with an ohmmeter, place the range on the R X 1 or R X 10 scale

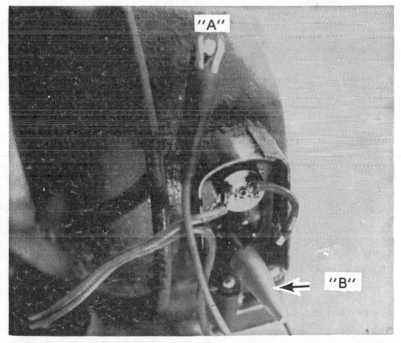

Fig. 5-3. An ohmmeter should be used to check a compressor for "grounds." Connect one lead to the compressor body (A) and the other to each of the motor terminals. There should be no meter indication in any case.

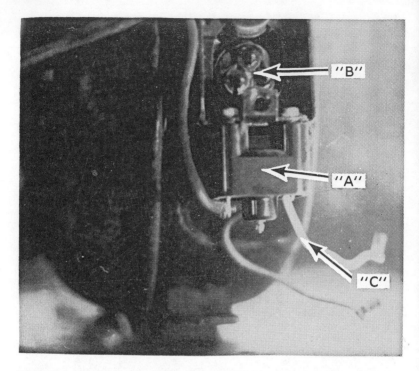

Fig. 5-4. Motor starting relay still mounted in its proper position (A). The motor terminals are at (B). The start and run connections with slip on terminals are shown at (C). These two wires have been disconnected from the terminals at (B) so that the windings of the compressor motor can be checked with an ohmmeter.

and connect the ohmmeter leads across the capacitor. The ohmmeter should deflect virgorously, then slowly fall back toward infinity. Now, reverse the ohmmeter test leads and you should again get the same effect. If the meter does not deflect or deflects a very small amount, or if it deflects all the way to zero and stays there, the capacitor should be replaced.

Some freezers and refrigerators do not have a motor-starting capacitor. If there is no capacitor or if the capacitor checks okay, the compressor should be checked next. Remove the relay leads from the compressor and check with an ohmmeter between each motor lead and the compressor body or

frame. There should be no reading. If there is, it is an indication of a ground in the unit (Fig. 5-3).

The next check is of the motor windings inside the compressor. There are three motor terminals and each should
read continuity to the others (Fig. 5-4). If the ohmmeter does
not read (does not move off infinity) between any two terminals one of the windings is open. Fig. 5-5 shows typical
ohmmeter readings at the compressor terminals. Fig. 5-6 is a
wiring diagram for a typical compressor motor. Notice that
the highest ohmmeter reading indicates you are checking
across both the run and start windings. The run winding
usually has the least resistance because it is wound with
larger wire than the start winding.

STARTING THE COMPRESSOR MOTOR MANUALLY

During normal operation the compressor motor is started
automatically by the starting relay which connects a
capacitor in series with the start winding for a short while,
then disconnects the capacitor after the motor attains about
three-fourths normal speed. A good way to check both the
compressor motor and the relay (by elimination) is the
method shown in Fig. 5-7. Make up a line cord and fuse combination as shown (a waterproof pigtail lamp socket makes a
good fuseholder) and connect it to the run winding terminals of
the compressor. (The arrangement of terminals might not
always be as shown, so check the windings with an ohmmeter;
the lowest resistance winding is the run winding.) Obtain a
capacitor of the size used with the compressor motor (for test
purposes the exact size is not mandatory) and clip it from the
hot side of the run winding to the hot side of the start winding.
(The hot side of the winding is the end of the winding not
connected to the other winding, as for example C and B in Fig.
5-6. Terminal A is called "common" since it has a common
connection to both windings.)

Plug the compressor in; if it is okay, the compressor
should start running; after a couple of seconds disconnect the
starting capacitor. The compressor should continue to speed
up and run normally. The above procedure accomplishes
manually what is normally performed automatically by the
motor starting relay. If you do not have a capacitor, you can
often get the compressor motor to start by just placing a wire
jumper momentarily across the terminals where the
capacitor is shown connected in Fig. 5-7; if the compressor
starts, disconnect the jumper as soon as the motor starts.

125

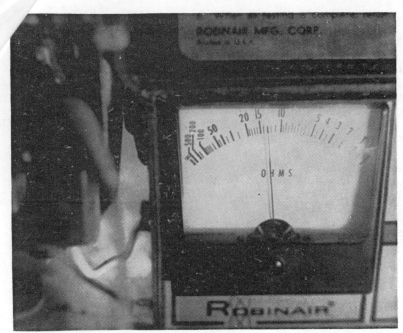

A

B

While leads are connected, rotate ZERO A
cates zero ohms.

4. Separate test leads and connect across
5. Read ohms scale on meter and multiply by
6. When all testing is complete, return range in
ROBINAIR MFG. CORP.
P.   N U.S.A.

C

Fig. 5-5 Checking compressor motor windings with an
ohmmeter. The resistance (A) between the start and run
terminals is the highest reading, since both windings are
being read in series (See Fig. 5-6). The resistance (B) of
the run winding only should be the least, since the run
winding is wound with heavier wire. The start winding
resistance is somewhere in between (C). If the ohmmeter
pointer had failed to move in any one of these tests, it
would have indicated a defective winding. However,
shorted turns in a winding may cause the motor to
overheat, while the defect goes undetected by an ohmmeter.

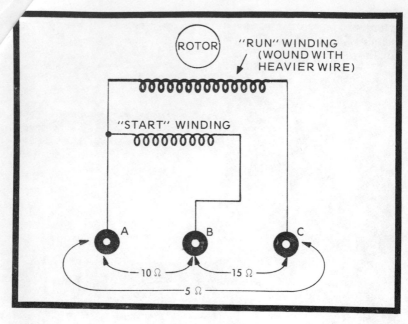

Fig. 5-6. Wiring diagram of a typical compressor motor.

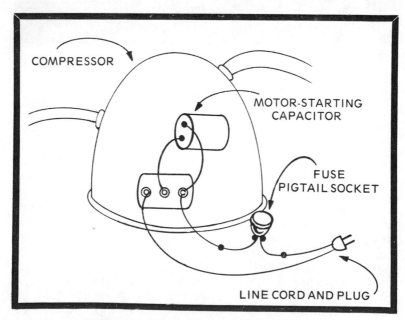

Fig. 5-7. Using the test line cord shown, it is possible to start the compressor manually if it is not defective.

Don't leave the jumper connected for more than a very few seconds or the starting winding inside the compressor can be destroyed.

USING A STARTER BOX

Special test starter boxes are available, such as shown in Fig. 5-8. This box is a bit more convenient than the method just described because it has a built-in line cord, fuse, various size motor-starting capacitors, and a pushbutton for temporarily connecting the capacitor during starting. The box also has indicator lights to check for shorts etc.

Fig. 5-8. A manual motor starting box. A pushbutton is used to temporarily connect the correct size capacitor into the start-winding circuit. Lights on the unit indicate shorts. Once the compressor is running, an ammeter will indicate current flow. If current is high, the motor will overheat and likely will not have enough power.

"Frozen" Or "Stuck" Compressor

When the compressor motor refuses to start because it is mechanically "locked," it usually means that you must replace the compressor unit; however, since the compressor is of no value anyway, you may want to try a "shock" treatment to see if you can get the motor turning again. Here's how:

Use the same system as shown in Fig. 5-7, except use a higher voltage capacitor if possible and connect the power line to 220 volts instead of 110. USE EXTREME CARE WHEN DOING THIS SO THAT YOU DO NOT COME IN CONTACT WITH THE 220 VOLTS—IT CAN KILL INSTANTLY. Sometimes the higher voltage will get the compressor turning, then it will start normally on its regular 110 volts. Don't leave the compressor running on 220 volts after it starts or it will soon become overheated and burn up the windings.

Sometimes a compressor won't start because it has high head pressure. In this case the refrigerator system must be checked with gauges as discussed in Chapter 5.

MOTOR-STARTING RELAYS

If you find by elimination that the motor-starting relay is defective, it should be replaced by one of the exact same type. There are several different types of relays, some with built-in protection against overload. The "hot wire" and "current" relay types are found only on older refrigerators, while "voltage" relays are used on newer refrigerators and freezers. Fig. 5-9 is a "hot wire" relay which uses a heated wire to open the contacts that switch the starting capacitor into the circuit. A second or two after the motor starts, the heat-sensitive wire expands and pulls the points open. When the motor stops the wire cools and the points go back together, ready for another starting cycle.

The "current" relay operates on the high current drawn when a motor is first turned on. The starting current, which is much higher than the running current, pulls in the motor relay that connects the capacitor into the circuit. As the motor approaches operating speed, the current decreases and the motor-starting relay "falls out," opening the switch and disconnecting the motor-starting capacitor. The disadvantage of this type relay is that the points close when current is applied, so there is some arcing at the switch contacts which reduces the life of the relay points. Fig. 5-10 is a simplified wiring diagram of a typical "current" motor-starting relay.

Fig. 5-9. A "hot wire" relay shown from both terminal and cover sides. Terminal A connects to the run winding and Terminal B to the start winding. The actual markings on the relay are generally "S" which goes to the start winding and "M" (for main) which goes to the run winding.

Notice that the points are normally open. However, when current is first applied to the motor, the relay pulls in quickly, then drops out when the current falls as the motor gains speed. Fig. 5-11 shows just some of the many varied housings used with current relays. Fig. 5-12 shows a current relay wiring diagram where no starting capacitor is used. Most current relays must be mounted in the correct position, since the points fall open due to gravity. Fig. 5-13 is a motor-starting relay with "slip on" terminals and overload protection all in one package.

The "voltage" or "potential" relay is the most popular type relay and it is found on later model refrigerators and freezers. The relay coil, unlike the "current" type, has many turns of wire. Fig. 5-14 is one type of potential relay. A simplified wiring diagram of a "potential" relay motor-starting system is shown in Fig. 5-15. The relay operates when the voltage rises across the coil, opening the points and taking the starting capacitor and winding out of the circuit. When the motor is first turned on, it draws heavy current so the voltage drop across the start winding is low (most of the voltage is

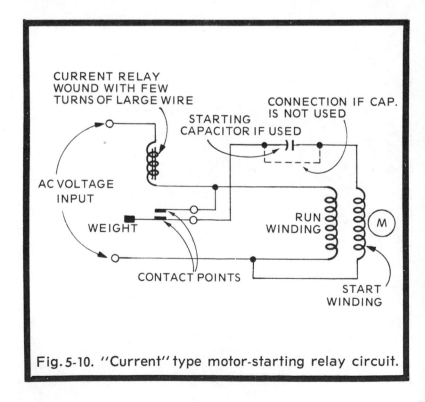

Fig. 5-10. "Current" type motor-starting relay circuit.

Fig. 5-11. Several types of "current" relays. Current relays are connected in series with a motor winding. Each has a few turns of heavy wire on the coil and is tripped by the heavy starting current of the motor. The relay drops out when the motor current decreases as the motor gains speed.

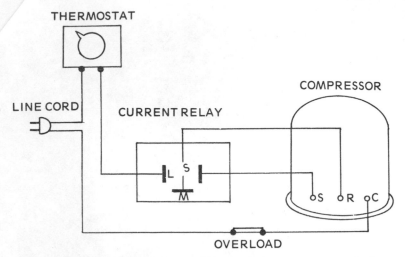

Fig. 5-12. This current relay motor-starting circuit does not use a capacitor.

Fig. 5-13. Current type motor-starting relay with slip-on terminals and built-in overload protector.

Fig. 5-14. A "potential" or "voltage" motor-starting relay. When the relay is defective, you should normally use an exact replacement; however, it may be possible to use a different type. Check with the wholesale supplier for a suitable substitute. Starting relays are rated in horse-power. The information stamped on the cover will enable you to find a replacement. If there is an arrow on the cover, it must point up when mounted.

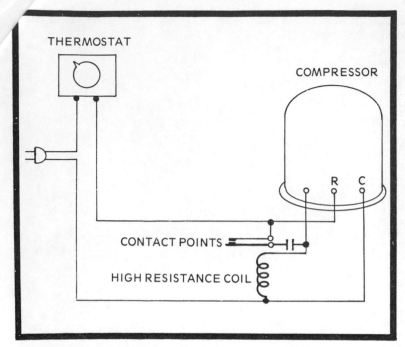

THERMOSTAT

COMPRESSOR

R C

CONTACT POINTS

HIGH RESISTANCE COIL

Fig. 5-15. Diagram of a start circuit using a "voltage" or "potential" relay.

across the capacitor), but as the motor picks up speed, there is less and less load and, consequently, more and more voltage induced into the start winding, so that finally the voltage rises enough (at about three-fourths full speed) so that the relay coil pulls the contacts open and takes the start winding out of the circuit. Even with the start winding disconnected from the power line, a voltage is induced in it by transformer action from the run winding, so the relay stays energized and keeps the start winding and capacitor disconnected. The points in this relay are closed when the current is high and open when the current is low, so point wear is good. A disadvantage is that a starting capacitor must be used. But the starting capacitor is a good idea in any event since it provides more starting torque than is attainable from comparable motors without it.

OVERLOAD PROTECTORS

Several different types of overload protectors are used. The purpose of the overload protector, of course, is to prevent damage to the compressor motor when trouble occurs, such as an open starting capacitor or a defective motor-starting relay, or if the compressor is overloaded due to high head pressure. Overloads automatically reset; that is, they will "click" out during an overload, then when cooled they will "click" in again and try to start the motor. If the problem still exists, the high current flow will open the relay again, etc. The cycle continues repeating until the motor starts, the power is turned off, or something burns out. The overloads work because of the considerably increased current drawn by a motor that doesn't start turning immediately. To prevent the overload from opening due to the high current when the motor is first turned on, even though operating normally, there is a thermal delay. In other words, the overload protector depends on a rise in temperature to operate. The high current of a normally starting motor will not produce enough heat to trip the protector, since it diminishes rapidly as the motor speeds up, but if the motor does not start, the heat increases in a few seconds to a point where the overload protection is activated. Most overload protectors have a disc-like diaphragm made of two different metals welded together. As the diaphragm is

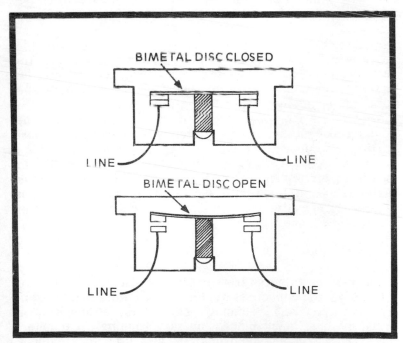

Fig. 5-16. A bimetal disc overload protector is opened when the disc is heated to a predetermined point.

Fig. 5-17. This small overload protector is used in some refrigerator and freezer units.

heated, the two metals expand at different rates, causing the diaphragm to warp (much like pushing in the bottom of a tin can) and pull two switch contacts apart, turning off the current to the motor. When the disc cools, it snaps back and closes the points again. See Fig. 5-16.

Fig. 5-17 is one type of overload protector. Sometimes, as indicated earlier, the overload protector is a part of the motor-starting relay. In addition to protecting the motor against high current flow, the overload is often situated so that it will also open if the motor-compressor temperature rises too high, as might happen if the compressor were overloaded but not sufficiently to cause the protector to open on the basis of current flow alone.

CAPACITORS

As may be gathered from preceding discussions, the two general types of capacitors used in refrigerators and freezers are "starting" and "running" capacitors, although little emphasis has been placed on a "running" capacitor. However, a "running" capacitor is also used to provide a "smoother" and quieter operating motor. It is permanently connected in the circuit between the hot sides of the start and run windings in the same electrical location as the start capacitor, as you can see in Fig. 5-18.

The running capacitor is always considerably smaller in electrical size than the starting capacitor; for example, the running capacitor might be 4 microfarads while the starting capacitor might be 180 microfarads. Capacitors are rated both in microfarads (MFD, mfd, or ufd) and in voltage. When replacing a capacitor you should stay within about 10 percent or so of the mfd rating and the voltage rating should be the same or higher. For example, a 180-mfd 200-volt capacitor could be replaced with a 200-mfd 220-volt capacitor, or with a 170-mfd capacitor at 250 volts. As a general rule, if the capacity is lower, the voltage rating will be higher. This is because more voltage is dropped across a smaller capacitor since it has a higher reactance (higher resistance to the flow of alternating current).

Starting capacitors are often housed in a plastic case, while running capacitors more often are housed in a metal can. In an emergency, where the right capacitor is not available as a replacement, you can use two or more

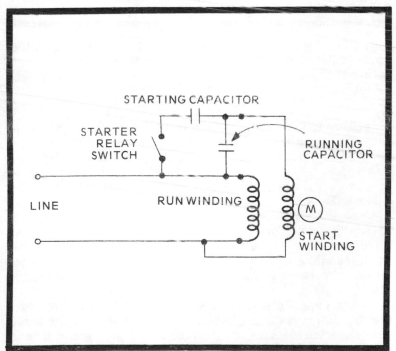

Fig. 5-18. This simplified schematic shows the position of the "running" capacitor in the circuit.

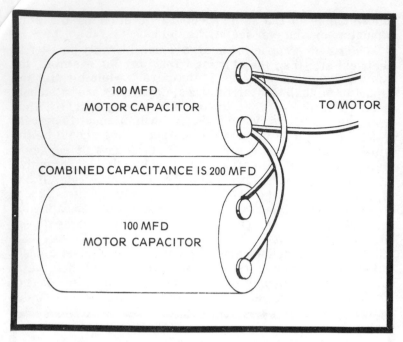

Fig. 5-19. Capacitors in parallel have a combined value equal to the sum of the individual capacitors. The voltage rating of the combination, however, is equal to the **lowest** voltage rating in the group.

capacitors either in series or parallel to produce the same electrical value (or one near enough) to work satisfactorily.

When you parallel capacitors, as shown in Fig. 5-19, the mfd values are added; that is, two 100-mfd capacitors in parallel will have a combined value of 200 mfd. And the capacitors do not have to be the same size; for example, you can parallel 50-mfd and a 100-mfd capacitors to get 150 mfd. The voltage rating of the parallel group is the same at the least rated capacitor. For example, three capacitors in parallel, one a 150-mfd at 220 volts, one a 50-mfd at 280 volts and a 25-mfd at 330 volts would have a combined rating of 225 mfd at 220 volts.

When capacitors are connected in series, as in Fig. 5-20, the calculation is more complex. Two capacitors of the same size connected in series, say, two 200-mfd capacitors, will have half the capacity rating or 100 mfd. The voltage ratings in this case are additive; that is, if both are rated at 150 volts, the two in series will have a total voltage rating of 300 volts. But what about capacitors in series that do not have the same rating? Take for example, a 200 mfd capacitor in series with a 100 mfd. If we call the 200-mfd capacitor "C1" and the 100-mfd capacitor "C2," here is the formula for working out the composite capacity:

$$\frac{C1 \ X \ C2}{C1 \ + \ C2}$$

Using the above values:

$$\frac{200 \ X \ 100}{200 \ + \ 100} = \frac{20,000}{300} = 66.66 \ \text{mfd}$$

What about the voltage rating? Let's say both have the same voltage rating of 200 volts. Will the composite voltage rating be 400 volts? No. The voltage rating must be calculated considering the relative size of the two capacitors. The smallest value capacitor will have the highest voltage across it. In this

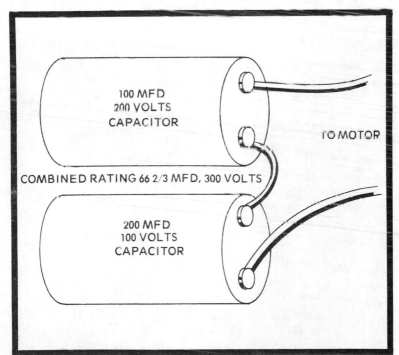

Fig. 5-20. Capacitors connected in series have a lower combined capacitor but a higher overall voltage rating.

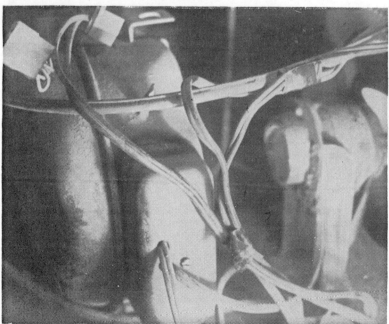

Fig. 5-21. A typical condenser fan motor and a typical freezer installation.

case the 100-mfd capacitor will have twice the voltage across it in the circuit as will the 200-mfd. The 100-mfd capacitor has a maximum rating at 200 volts; therefore, since it will always have twice as much voltage across it as the 200-mfd capacitor we can put only 300 volts total across the combination. In other words, 300 volts applied will put 200 volts across the 100-mfd capacitor and 100 volts across the 200-mfd. The above calculations are for AC voltages, and since motor-starting and running capacitors are always rated in AC voltage, this is the only calculation necessary. Looking at the above calculations, you can see that it would be possible to get a 66 2/3-mfd capacitor with a 300-volt rating by series connecting a 100-mfd capacitor with a 200-volt rating and a 200-mfd capacitor with a 100 volt-rating.

CHANGING THERMOSTATS

When changing thermostats, it is a good idea to mark the leads and make sure they are returned to the same terminals on the new one. A thermostat has only two terminals and as far as the refrigerator is concerned the wires could be reversed to the unit and the thermostat would still work. But often the thermostat is a junction point for the light, defrosting heaters, etc. If you install a new thermostat and find that the light comes on when the door is opened only with the unit running, you have gotten one of the wires to the thermostat on the wrong side. If the unit runs all the time, check the wiring. It is likely that the thermostat has been wired so that the unit is connected directly to the power line or perhaps through a heater to the power line. Moral: A bit of time to mark which wires connect together at which thermostat terminal will pay big dividends and save lots of frustration.

CONDENSER FAN MOTORS

Refrigerators and freezers use condenser fan motors of different types. Most are shaded pole, fractional horsepower types. A typical condenser fan and motor is shown in Fig. 5-21. These small motors are often called "throwaway" motors, since it is normally more economical and practical to replace the motor with a new one rather than try to repair the old for any except the most minor external troubles. Such motors are usually pre-oiled, then pressed together and sealed so that no dirt can get inside. Replacement motors are available for either clockwise or counterclockwise rotation as needed and for either 110 or 220 volts AC. If you should decide to repair a condenser fan motor, it will look something like the one shown disassembled in Fig. 5-22.

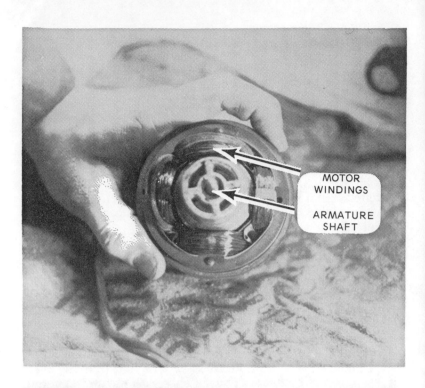

MOTOR
WINDINGS

ARMATURE
SHAFT

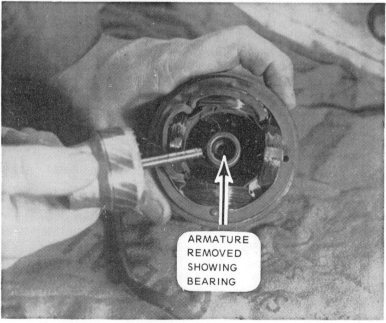

ARMATURE
REMOVED
SHOWING
BEARING

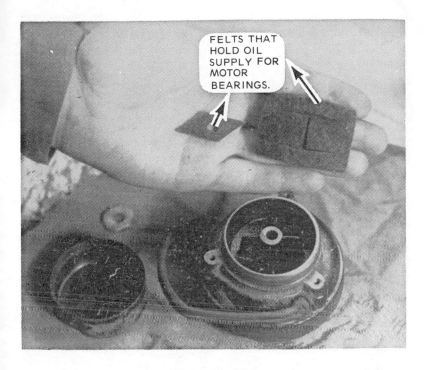

Fig. 5-22. A condenser fan motor in various stages of disassembly.

Checking A Fan Motor

A fan motor can be checked for several defects, but the serviceman must use a bit of judgment as to the feasibility repair. First a motor may have lost its lubrication (dry of oil) and the bearings have tightened up, thus preventing the armature shaft from turning. A shaded-pole motor has very little starting torgue, so any drag on the shaft can easily prevent it from rotating. If the motor shaft seems to spin freely, the problem is likely an electrical one. Check with a voltmeter to make sure that the voltage reaching the motor is correct; if so, disconnect the power and check the windings for continuity with an ohmmeter. Also check between the motor windings

Fig. 5-23. Ohmmeter shows continuity of the winding in a fan motor.

and the frame of the motor for a possible short or leakage (use the R X 100 or a higher scale for this last test).

Fig. 5-23 shows an ohmmeter check of a winding (use the R X 1 scale for this test). If the winding measures open and if the external leads are okay, the best idea is to replace the entire motor with a new one. This is true, also, if the windings indicate a leakage or if there is a short between the winding and the motor frame.

Still another way to check a motor is a "dynamic" test using a set of jumper leads as in Fig. 5-24 to connect directly from the motor leads to the power line. This method gives a positive indication of the motor's condition and bypasses any other electrical circuits that might be at fault rather than the motor. If the motor runs when a jumper is attached and won't run when connected in the refrigerator or freezer circuit, the problem is clearly not in the motor but in some part of the wiring or switches.

146

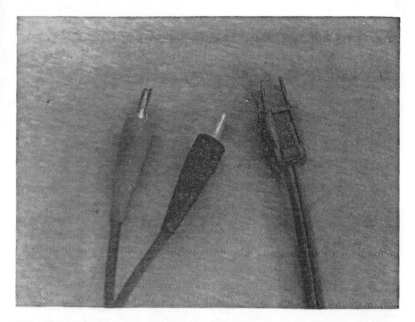

Fig. 5-24. A "jumper" cord, with insulated alligator clips on one end and a suitable AC power plug on the other, can be used to temporarily apply power to a motor for tests. Take care when using a cord of this sort that you do not touch the bare clips when they're hot!

If oiling is all that is necessary to get the motor operating again, you can oil a sealed motor by punching a hole in each bearing housing and forcing oil in it. Solder the hole shut so that dirt won't accumulate inside the motor and again "freeze" the motor shaft.

Chapter 6

Dishwashers

Though much alike in many respects, there are a number of types of dishwashers in use. There are dishwashers, for example, that prerinse dishes and hold them for washing later. The purpose of this function, of course, is to prevent food from drying on the dishes. For dishwashers that do not have this feature, dishes can be prerinsed by hand before placing them in the dishwasher. Of course, if dishes are to be washed immediately, they may not need prerinsing. Many modern-day dishwashers operate with such high pressure that even dried-on food will be swept away. Some also have a heater which increases the temperature of the dishwasher considerably beyond that of the hot water used in the home. Another feature in some is an extra "sterilizing" cycle which forces hot fresh water through the dishes just prior to the drying cycle.

In a dishwasher the timer is one of the most important parts and the part that often gives the most trouble. The timer controls the various functions—turning the water off and on, preheating the water, pumping the water in and out, etc.

PORTABLE & BUILT-IN DISHWASHERS

Two general cabinet types are used for dishwashers, portable and built-in. Some portable types can be built in if you wish but they may be stored out of sight when not in use. Portable dishwashers require water hoses with disconnects that are attached to a faucet equipped with a hose bib and to a drain. On occasion special plumbing is provided for portable dishwashers, but there should always be a shut-off valve prior to the hose connection in case repairs are needed.

Special fittings are available to connect the hoses to faucets without hose bibs. Fig. 6-1 shows one type, dual-hose connection in which the top hose is used to carry hot water to the dishwasher and the bottom hose serves a drain that allows the used water to fall into the sink.

Fig. 6-1. A drain-fill 2-hose fitting often used with portable dishwashers.

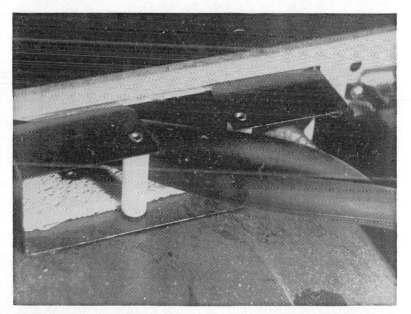

Fig. 6-2. Storage compartment on a typical portable dishwasher for hoses and power cord.

Fig. 6-3. The lower plastic impeller on a typical dish-washer. Water is forced through the impeller. The im-peller showers water over the dishes, loosening and flushing away the food particles. The impeller spins because of the force of the water escaping through the holes; therefore, it should spin easily on its shaft. You can remove the impeller by loosening a snap ring or nut, or in some cases by simply lifting it straight up. The rod-type ring underneath the impeller is the water heater element which further increases the hot water temperature to "sterilize" dishes.

If the portable dishwasher has a heating element, it may blow the fuse when plugged into an existing circuit. In this case a separate circuit should be provided with ample size wire and protection to take care of the maximum dishwasher load. The nameplate on the dishwasher will give you the total current drawn by the unit. The circuit should be fused around 50 percent above the normal load when using a slow blow fuse or a circuitbreaker. For "quick blow" fuses, the rating may have to be 100 percent above so as to allow for starting surges, etc. In other words, if the dishwasher draws 10 amperes maximum, the fuse may have to be 20 amperes. For a 20 ampere circuit, the wiring should be at least no. 12 wire. **Do not overfuse a circuit just to keep the fuse from blowing. This creates a possible fire hazard since the wiring may be too small to carry the additional load without overheating.**

Fig. 6-2 shows the storage area on one type of portable dishwasher where the water hoses and the electrical cord can be stored.

Fig. 6-3 shows a ring-type water heating element and an impeller which is free to spin as water is pumped through it. The water forced through the impeller showers hot, soapy water over the dishes as it turns. The small circuit near the bottom of the picture is the water level control; it is not used on all dishwashers. Fig. 6-4 shows the impeller removed. Most impellers can be slipped off by pulling sharply upward; others, however, may have a nut or lock ring to hold them in

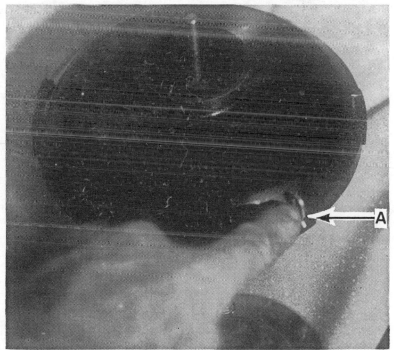

Fig. 6-4. After lifting off the impeller, the plastic housing can be removed for cleaning or repair. In this case, a cotter pin is removed at "A," then the housing is turned clockwise for removal.

Fig. 6-5. This photo shows the underneath side of the housing being removed in Fig. 6-4. The finned metal plate here does **not** turn but is used to direct the water coming from the pump impeller. Occasionally, for cleaning, the nut at the center will have to be removed and the finned plate taken out.

place. The impeller should spin freely when tapped with your finger. If impeller movement is sluggish the dishwasher will not likely do a thorough job.

In the dishwasher shown in Fig. 6-4, a cotter pin must be removed before the housing under the impeller can be removed. The housing covers the water pump which forces the water up and through the external impeller. To loosen the pump impeller housing, it may be necessary to use a small punch and hammer to force the housing to turn. In this dishwasher the housing must turn clockwise to loosen. To loosen it, however, you may have to tap it first one way then the other to break up deposits which may interfere with removal.

The underneath side of the pump impeller housing is shown in Fig. 6-5. The metal plate shown does not turn but simply directs the water; sometimes, though, the metal plate must be removed so you can clean out the holes and allow the water to flow freely again.

Fig. 6-6 is a view of the pump impeller, which can be removed by loosening the stud on the shaft (you will need to prevent the impeller from turning so the stud can be loosened). It is necessary to remove the impeller when a complete cleaning of the pump system is needed. Fig. 6-7 shows a repairman removing the impeller so that foreign material in the pump can be cleared away.

In some dishwashers the impeller has movable blades or fins which sling out as the motor runs. If the pump is not forcing out enough water, check these blades to make sure they are not "stuck." Usually, they can be "unstuck" with just

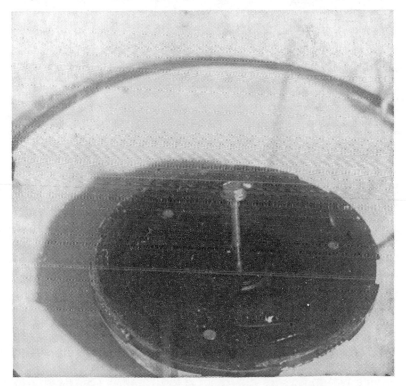

Fig. 6-6. This is the pump impeller. To remove it, use a screwdriver to block it from turning, then loosen the center stud. Care should be taken not to break the impeller while trying to loosen the nut.

soap and hot water. They should, though, move freely without any binding before reassembling the pump. If one or more impeller blades are broken, it will be necessary to replace the entire impeller assembly. Be sure to order by dishwasher make and model numbers, which can be found on the nameplate normally mounted on the back or along the front at the bottom of the dishwasher.

When doing a complete cleaning job, you will have to remove the other side of the housing, as shown in Fig. 6-8, to get to the screen that keeps foreign material out of the pump. If this screen is clogged, not enough water can get through and the dishwasher will not clean the dishes properly. To prevent clogging, many dishwasher manufacturers urge that large

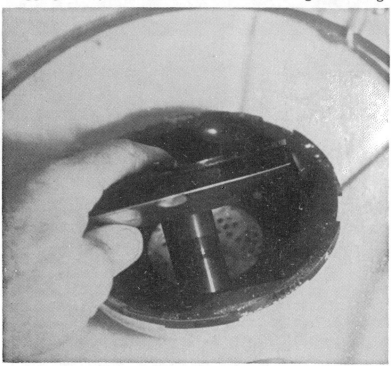

Fig. 6-7. Removing the pump impeller to allow cleaning foreign material from the pump. Such cleaning is necessary whenever it becomes clogged to the point where water flow is cut down significantly. Some pump impellers have small blades which sling outward as the impeller turns; if you encounter this type, be sure the blades are free to move. If they stick, the dishwasher will not get the dishes clean.

amounts of food be cleaned off before the dishes are placed into the dishwasher. Some dishwashers, however, are made to process more residual food without clogging than others. Generally, if the dishwasher is an older model, you should always rinse away all excess food before placing the dishes in the dishwasher.

Gaining access to the inside of portable dishwashers may require the removal of the top. Usually, this is a matter of taking out two or more screws, or it may be held in place with snaps or catches. Often, you need to remove perhaps two screws, then pull the top sharply toward the front to release horizontal catches.

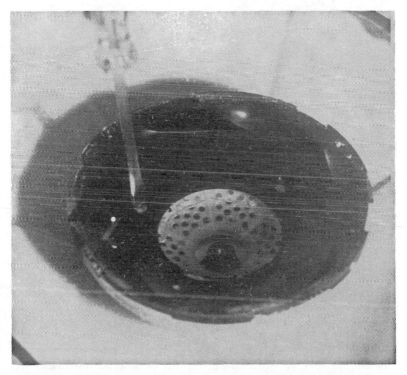

Fig. 6-8. The repairman is removing the screws so the other half of the housing can be taken out to allow access to the strainer or screen below. The strainer prevents foreign material from reaching the pump, especially food and other particles from the dishes. If this strainer is clogged, not enough water will flow and the dishes will be poorly cleaned.

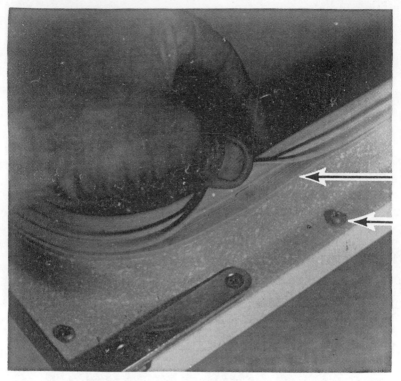

Fig. 6-9. Dishwasher door gaskets are attached by clips or screws.

LEAKING AROUND DOOR GASKET

If water leaks out on the floor when the dishwasher runs, it may be caused by a defective door gasket. Inspect the gasket to see if it still has a "rubbery" feel and no creases or tears. To remove and replace a door gasket, you will either have to remove screws, clips or both (Fig. 6-9). Order a new gasket by make and model number.

If the gasket is okay, it may be that the door latch is not working properly. You can tighten the door latch normally by moving the catch, which is often mounted with two screws through slotted holes. Often only a slight tightening is all that is needed to stop the leaks. If you get the latch too tight, the door will be hard to close and you may even squeeze the gasket out of shape and create another leak. In most dishwashers, the unit will not run until the door has been securely latched. Fig. 6-10 shows a typical dishwasher door latch.

TIMER

On many dishwashers the timer is mounted inside the door. But wherever the timer is mounted, you almost always have to remove a panel to expose the wiring and the mechanism. If the timer is at fault, be sure to replace it with one made for the make and model in question. As on washing machines, timers are not interchangeable.

Checking The Timer

After getting into the timer, checking is easier if you have a wiring diagram so you can determine where each terminal connects to the respective parts. However, if you do not have a wiring diagram, you can still check the timer by tracing the wiring from the malfunctioning part of the dishwasher to the timer. For example, if the motor does not start, find the lead which runs from the motor to the timer. Next, find the lead that comes from the power line to the timer. Be sure the power

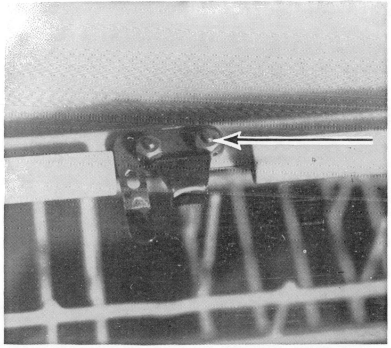

Fig. 6-10. Typical dishwasher door latch.

line is disconnected, then unplug the wires from the timer lugs. Use an ohmmeter or a continuity test lamp across these terminals (Fig. 6-11). The ohmmeter should read or the test lamp light as you rotate the timer switch. If it doesn't, the internal switch mechanism is defective and it will be necessary to replace the complete timer.

Be sure, if you remove more than two leads (or even if only two leads, it's still a good idea), to mark them or make a record of the colors so that you won't make a mistake in getting them back correctly. **Don't try to remember, since you will almost surely forget if you need a little extra time for tracing or if you are temporarily interrupted. Mark the leads! It's much too embarrassing if you forget.**

Remember that on some timers it is necessary to pull out or push in the knob to start the operation (Fig. 6-12). A customer will find it difficult to forgive you if you can't figure

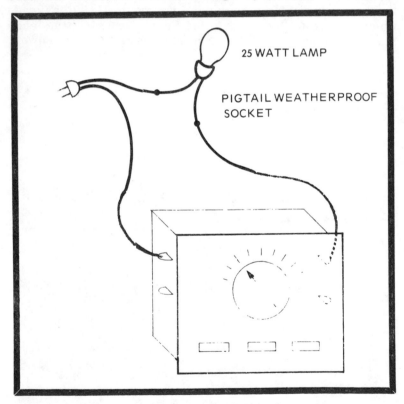

25 WATT LAMP

PIGTAIL WEATHERPROOF SOCKET

Fig. 6-11. A 110v test lamp can be used to check switch contacts inside the timer. Be sure power to the dishwasher is disconnected.

out how to get the machine turned on! She won't be able to imagine how anyone could possibly fix a machine he doesn't even know how to turn on. Remember also that the door latch must be fully closed before the machine will start. It sometimes happens that the door latch appears to close okay but still doesn't trip the safety switch. Remove whatever panels are necessary to take a look at the switch and see whether or not it is being activated. Check it also for continuity with either your ohmmeter or test lamp. Note: Never check continuity with either an ohmmeter or test lamp when the power is turned on. Make double sure the power is disconnected from both sides of the line. Pull the plug, or if there is no plug, remove the power line wires at the input terminals before making checks.

HEATING ELEMENT

Fig. 6-13 is a picture of the heating element terminals on the bottom of the dishwasher. Remove one of the leads (they

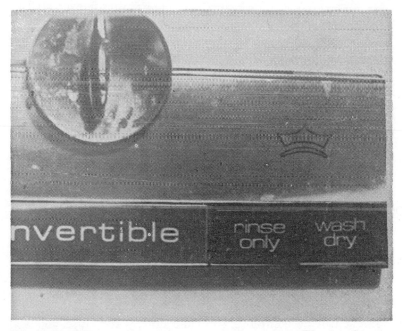

Fig. 6-12. Timer controls on one dishwasher. The knob sets the time cycles, while pushbuttons select the rinse or complete wash-dry operation.

Fig. 6-13. The water heating element terminals are on the bottom of the dishwasher. Usually, the connections are slip-on types.

normally plug on) and check across the element with an ohmmeter or test lamp. The element should have continuity; that is, the meter should read or the test lamp should light.

You can also check the heating element "live" with an AC ammeter, such as the "clip-on" discussed in Chapter 2. A heating element will usually draw in the neighborhood of 6 to 10 amperes, but normally it will draw either a significant amount or nothing at all, depending upon whether it is good or bad. It is rare to find a heating element that has a lower than or a higher than normal current drain; in just about all cases they will be completely good or completely bad.

In a few cases you may find a heating element that has shorted to ground, but usually if the short develops the element will be completely burned out by the time you are called; however, if you see an element which appears to have been overheated on one side only, you can suspect a shorted one. Remove both leads from the element and check from each terminal to the metal case of the dishwasher—you should get no continuity on either lead.

DRAIN INOPERATIVE

This is most often caused by a restriction in the drain hose. It may be due to the presence of foreign material in the drain hose, but it's more likely to be a "kinked" hose. Check to be sure that the hose makes no sharp bends on its way from the dishwasher to the drain.

If the drain is attached to the garbage disposer, make sure that the knockout plug in the side of the disposer has been cleanly removed before attaching the drain hose. If the dish-

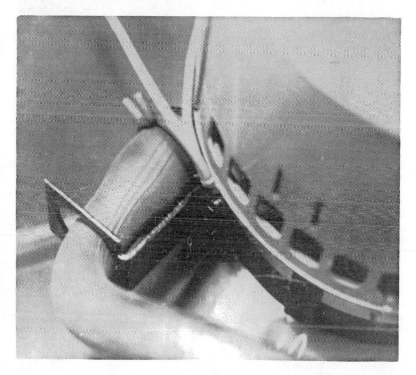

Fig. 6-14. Drain hose leaving pump. Notice that the hose is retained by a spring hose clamp. Special hose-clamp pliers are available for removing and replacing such clamps. Generally, though, they are fairly easy to remove with an ordinary pair of pliers but may be extremely difficult to replace, especially if located in a "tight" place. If the drain hose becomes kinked or clogged, water may be left in the dishwasher after the drying cycle is finished.

Fig. 6-15. Motor-starting relay used on some dishwashers.

washer is operating correctly, it should be completely free of standing water when the timer shuts off the machine after washing.

Another reason that the water may not all be pumped out is an obstruction in the drain hose. Remove the hose and check for foreign matter and also check inside the pump. Fig. 6-14 shows a drain hose connection to a pump. In some dishwashers, when the motor turns one direction it is washing dishes and when it turns in the other direction it pumps the water out the drain. Others have a solenoid valve in the drain, and so long as this valve is not activated, the water is forced up through the impeller blade and out over the dishes; when it's time to drain the water, the timer opens the drain valve and the water is pumped out by the same action used during the wash cycle.

MOTOR-STARTING RELAYS

Some dishwasher motors have a starting relay similar to the one shown in Fig. 6-15. This type relay has to be mounted in

Fig. 6-16. A solenoid water valve. This valve will allow water to flow through it when the coil around it is connected to 110 volts AC. Failure of valve to operate may be caused by an open coil, by defective timer switch, or by the plunger stuck open or closed.

the correct position or it will not work. When a motor-starting relay is used, it should pull in (snap closed) when the motor is first turned on, then fall out (snap open) as the motor gains speed (this should take no longer than a second or so).

If you can get to the coil terminals, check the relay for continuity. Also inspect the points to see whether or not they are severely pitted. Don't take chances when the relay is suspect—get the numbers from it and order a replacement. It is usually less expensive to replace the relay than to spend time trying to fix the old one—and almost invariably more satisfactory.

SOLENOID VALVES

Dishwashers use solenoid water valves almost identical to those found on washing machines (see Chapter 7). Fig. 6-16

Fig. 6-17. The holes in the impeller should be clear of foreign matter; otherwise, water flow will be restricted and dishes will not be washed properly.

shows a typical valve. When the timer contacts close, calling for water, 110 volts is applied to the solenoid which pulls in a plunger and opens the water line, allowing water to flow into the dishwater.

If the water doesn't get through the valve, listen for a click in the valve as the timer is turned. If you do not hear a click, either the solenoid coil is open or the timer is not supplying voltage to it. You can use an ohmmeter or test lamp to check the coil for continuity. If the coil doesn't appear to be open, check for voltage across the terminals with the dishwasher plugged in and the timer turned to the correct position. If there is no voltage, the timer is defective, a wire is broken, or there is no power coming into the dishwasher.

If a solenoid valve does not shut off the water, it is probably sticking and should be cleaned as explained in Chapter 7. Take care when you take the valve apart to protect the rubber gasket since the gasket can be used again if it is not torn up during disassembly.

IMPELLER

One of the causes of poor washing is due to the fact that water is not freely circulating through the impeller. Fig. 6-17, shows a typical impeller. Make sure that the holes in the impeller are not clogged. If they are, you can push out the foreign matter with an ice pick or something of that sort; be sure you flush away all the dirt, etc., by forcing water through the impeller. You can generally do a more thorough job of cleaning the impeller if you remove it from the shaft; however, that may not be necessary nor even desirable, especially if the impeller is difficult to remove.

Most all dishwashers have two impellers, one at the bottom and the other near the top. Fig. 6-18 shows the top impeller on one type of dishwasher. In other dishwashers, the top impeller is suspended from the top of the machine and the water is pumped up through tubing at the back and over the top into the impeller.

Fig. 6-18. Top circulating impeller may be mounted on a shaft coming out of the bottom as shown here, or it may be suspended from the top with water pumped to it from the bottom of the machine.

Chapter 7

Automatic Washers

Automatic clothes washers range from simple to complex. More complex machines have more cycles (wash, rinse, spin dry, etc.) and may have various water temperature settings. The timer is the heart of the automatic washer or, perhaps more correctly, the brain. It tells the machine what to do and when to do it. If troubles occur in the timer, the washing machine may operate erratically, stop during a cycle or function change, or refuse to work at all. Just about any automatic washer needs only one manual operation—turning on the timer. Once the timer is engaged, it takes over as an "automatic pilot," guiding the machine through filling, washing, rinsing, spin drying, and the like.

On filling, some automatic washers depend upon a time cycle. Therefore, for different levels of water pressure, it may be necessary for the housewife to set the timer at a predetermined spot to make sure the washer will get enough water without overfilling. Other washers have a water level control switch which holds the timer at the "fill" position until the water level reaches the correct point, then the timer automatically advances to the next function or cycle.

The second cycle is the "wash" function and the timer holds the machine in that position for a definite time. Most automatic washers use a back-and-forth agitator action during the wash interval to beat out the dirt; however, at least one major manufacturer uses an up-and-down agitator action. Upon completion of the wash cycle, the timer starts a "spin" cycle. Some washers pump out the wash water before the spin cycle begins, while others pump the water out as the spin cycle begins. Some washers are designed so that the drive motor runs in one direction for washing, then reverses when the spin cycle occurs. Motor reversal in these machines automatically locks the transmission gears into the spin cycle; reversing the motor again causes the transmission to operate the "agitator" cycle. Other machines do not reverse the motor but use an electrically operated solenoid lever to change the transmission function.

Once the spin cycle is finished, the tub stops rotating and clear, cold rinse water enters the tub through a solenoid water valve. Generally, the agitator is activated during the spin function to force the soapy wash water out of the clothes. Following this, the rinse water is pumped out and another spin-dry cycle occurs. Depending upon the washer, there may be one or even several rinse cycles before the final spin-dry cycle. During the spin-dry cycle, the tub rotates at high speed and literally "slings" the water out of the clothes. The water, of course, drains into the pump and is discharged.

In reality, there are two tubs in an automatic washer—an "outer" tub which holds water and does not rotate and an "inner" tub which is either full of holes, as in Fig. 7-1, or has

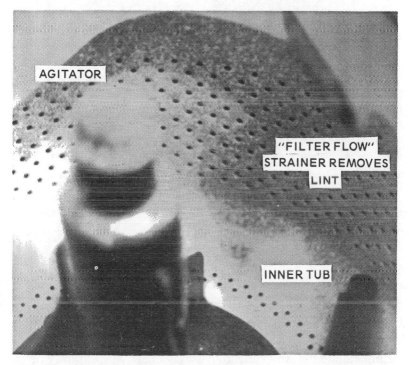

Fig. 7-1. The inner tub on an automatic washing machine generally has holes in the sides and bottom so that the water can be drained out while still holding the clothes in place. Some inner tubs have holes or slots only near the top and the water is thrown up and over during the spin cycle. In this machine a filter cleans the water as it is recirculated from the outer tub   back into the inner tub.

Fig. 7-2. One type of timer control with the "regular" wash cycles on one side and the "gentle" cycles on the other. The most common method of producing a "gentle" cycle is to slow down the drive motor on the washing machine.

holes near the top where the water is thrown out when the tub starts to spin. During the wash cycle the inner tub is locked in place.

THE TIMER

Normally the timer is located near the top of the washer, either at the back or up front; however, the most common place is on a raised apron at the top rear of the machine (Figs. 7-2 and 7-3). The timer is nearly always just behind the function knob, though in a few instances the control knob may be connected to the timer through a long shaft, since it may be at or near the bottom rear of the machine.

To gain access to the timer you may either have to pull off the back panel or you may have to remove the top of the machine (especially on front-loading machines). All timers have several wires connected to them, and it is highly important—unless you are completely familiar with the machine—that you do not take off any wires without marking where they go (Fig. 7-4). There may be a wiring diagram to go by, but even with a wiring diagram it can be a problem to get the wires back where they belong. The wires generally are of different colors and sometimes are numbered. In some cases the timer terminals are color-coded or marked, but make sure before you indiscriminately remove wires. Fig. 7-5 is an example of a sketch showing wire connections. It makes little difference how rough the drawing is, so long as you can interpret it after several days as you might have to wait for a part. Fig. 7-6 shows the specifications needed to order a replacement.

An AC jumper cord, as described earlier, provides a simple way to check the timer. Plug the cord into a power source, then connect it directly to the timer motor terminals (be sure to remove present leads first) to see whether or not the timer will run. If the timer runs when the power is connected directly and doesn't when the timer is turned to "fill," it could mean a defective fill switch. (The fill switch stops the timer until the water level is correct.) The fill switch is generally operated by the pressure in a rubber tube connected

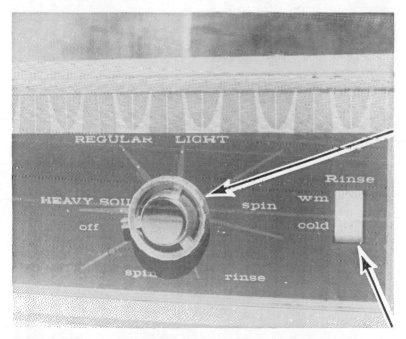

Fig. 7-3. This timer knob can be set for heavy, medium or light loads. The thumb switch to the right of the timer knob lets you select either a cold or warm rinse.

OPPOSITE SIDE OF TIMER

Fig. 7-4.

170

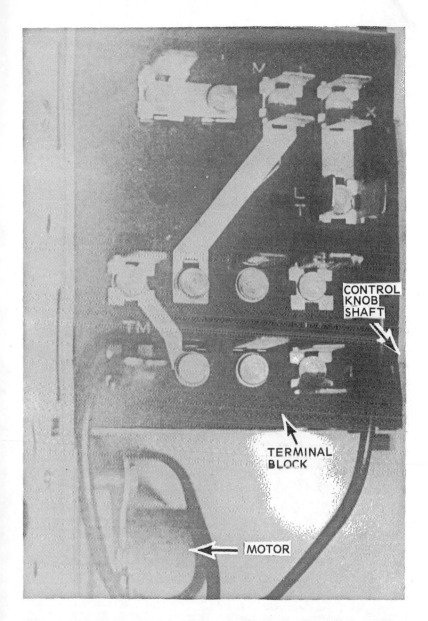

Fig. 7-4. An overall view of a typical washer timer. The terminals are generally lettered or numbered to show where the wires go; however, you should make sure of the correct placement of the wires by making yourself a small rough diagram (Fig. 7-5) whenever you have to remove more than one wire.

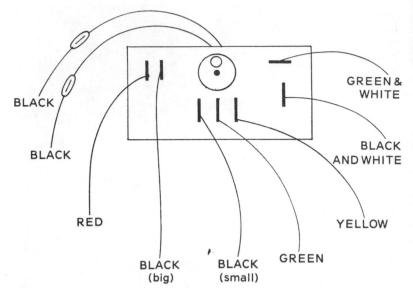

Fig. 7-5. A sketch of the connections to a typical timer. Such a drawing can save time when replacing a timer.

Fig. 7-6. The information needed to order a new timer is usually stamped on the cover.

to the bottom of the outer tub. When the weight of the water in the tube is sufficient it pushes on a diaphragm which in turn operates a switch to start the timer again and turns off the water inlet. Of course, this function does not exist in washers with a timed fill cycle.

Washers have a "temperature" switch which allows only the hot water inlet to open when the switch is turned to "hot." When the washer is set to "warm," both the cold and hot water inlet valves operate.

How The Timer Works

A clock motor in the timer is geared so that it will operate a number of switches in a predetermined sequence. The motor does not run when the timer is off. To initiate the wash cycle the timer is turned clockwise past the off position, or on many machines the timer is turned on either by pulling out or pushing in on the timer knob. The clock motor gearbox drives

Fig. 7-7. The timer motor actuates finger-type switches which control the various functions.

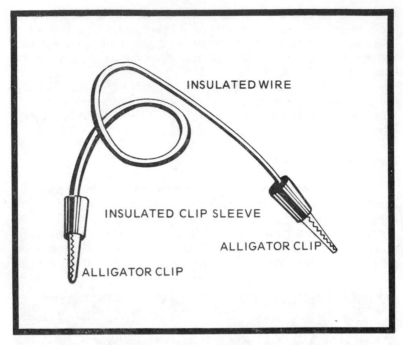

INSULATED WIRE

INSULATED CLIP SLEEVE

ALLIGATOR CLIP

ALLIGATOR CLIP

Fig. 7-8. A clip-clip jumper (a length of wire with an alligator clip on each end) is useful in bypassing switches.

a cam arrangement which pushes finger-type switches on and off to control the washer action. (Fig. 7-7.) If the washer runs but fails to operate on one or more of its various cycles, the trouble may be in the timer, but be sure that it is before you order a new timer—they are quite expensive. If, for example, the machine does not fill, check to see that voltage is reaching the solenoid coil of the water mixer valve; if it is, the timer is not at fault. If the wash cycle fails to start, see if the motor is getting power; also, determine if the fill safety switch is preventing power from reaching the timer motor when it shouldn't. Determine from the wiring diagram how you can bypass the timer switches so as to make sure that the timer really is at fault.

One rather common fault that may occur is a wire that has become disconnected, perhaps left insecurely attached either at the factory or during a previous repair. Make sure that all plugs are securely connected and pushed firmly in place. A clip-clip jumper or several of them like the one shown in Fig. 7-8 can be a big help in diagnosing possible troubles. Remember, though, that you must not get this jumper across a power source or you will immediately blow a fuse or breaker, or even worse cause damage to a timer switch.

In most cases you can tell whether the timer motor is running or not by looking through a small window on the back of the timer motor. If the motor is not running, it is not a definite indication that the motor is defective. It may mean that the timer switch is not turning on, or that some other switch or wire is not allowing voltage to reach the timer motor.

THE WASH CYCLE

When the timer moves to "wash," the drive motor applies power to the transmission. Most transmissions are enclosed, but in one major brand at least (Frigidaire) it is completely open. Sometimes there is a solenoid lever clutch which shifts the transmission into the right "gear." If a solenoid is used, you can hear it snap in when the wash cycle begins. Other machines simply start the motor; the change between wash and spin cycles is accomplished by reversing the motor.

THE SPIN CYCLE

After the first wash cycle the automatic washer goes into a "spin" cycle in which the inner tub slowly starts to revolve, gradually increasing in speed until it is spinning at several hundred revolutions a minute. This removes the water from the clothes by centrifugal force. The water is thrown into the outer tub where it is pumped into the drain. The pump is nearly always operated by the main drive motor through an extension shaft on the opposite end from the main drive pulley. Some model washers pump out the excess water before the inner tub starts to spin, while others start the entire water load into a spin. If the inner tub has water outlets only at the top, it must start spinning with the full water load. On models which use reverse motor action to switch between wash and spin, the pump may also be used to recirculate the washwater during the wash cycle and to pump out the water during the spin cycle.

As the spin cycle starts, a certain amount of "slippage" is necessary between the motor and the inner tub, otherwise the motor would not be strong enough to get the tub up to speed, or if it were, the tub would start spinning so quickly as to be detrimental. In many machines the slippage occurs in a slip clutch or simply in a V-belt drive. Because of this slippage, there naturally is excessive wear during the start of the spin

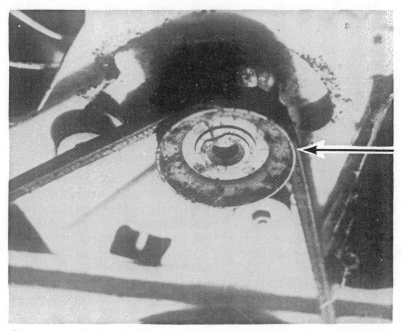

Fig. 7-9. A drive pulley on one make washing machine. If this pulley and the V belt should get wet or greasy, or if the belt is not tight enough, there will be too much slippage and the machine may not spin out the water properly. Or the water may spin out of the tub but the clothes may not be as dry as they normally would be.

cycle, and it is not at all unusual to find that one of the weak points in an automatic is the means of providing the necessary slip. If the tub will not start spinning or starts extremely slow, check the slip linkage, whatever it is (Fig. 7-9).

On washers with exposed gears (usually nylon plastic rollers rather than gears), grease or even soapy water will cause the rollers to slip, thereby impeding the spin action. Check for leaks under the washer and also for an over supply of oil. Remove the oil with a clean dry cloth or put a little alcohol on the cloth if absolutely necessary. Once the spin cycle starts, it will usually dry the roller sufficiently due to the heat generated by the slippage. Another cause of slow spin or no spin is an inner tub bearing that is frozen or binding. You should be able to turn the tub easily by hand when the timer is in the spin cycle. **Be careful not to get caught by the tub should it suddenly start to spin.**

Fig. 7-10 shows a washing machine motor that reverses between the wash and spin cycle. The giveaway to the use of a reversing motor is the number of wires connected to it. Only two or three are required for a nonreversing motor.

Automatic washer engineers approach various functions in many different ways, so what is an abnormal function on one machine may be a perfectly normal or intentional one on another. For example, some washers allow some water to run into the tub, through the clothes, and out again during the spin cycle, while others stop the tub and go through a complete agitator rinse cycle with the inner tube locked.

In most cases there is a brake to slow the tub down when the spin cycle shuts off. There are several braking methods. In some cases a solenoid lever holds the break off until the timer turns off the spin cycle; in others, the solenoid may pull the brake on when the timer signals the end of the spin cycle. Figs. 7-11, 7-12 and 7-13 are photos of braking systems.

Fig. 7-10. A washer motor that reverses between cycles usually has a number of wires connected to it.

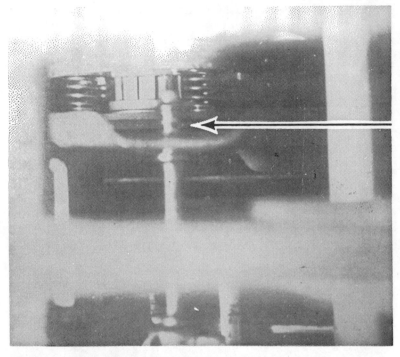

Fig. 7-11. One type of brake used on automatic washers. When the inner tub is spinning, the brake is released. When the spin cycle shuts off, the fiber brake material makes contact with a housing connected to the inner tub. The brake brings the inner tub to a stop and holds it in place during the wash or rinse cycles.

RINSE CYCLE

Most automatic washers have separate rinse cycles, even if they run water in and out during the spin cycle. The rinse cycle is almost identical to the wash cycle, except that no soap is added to the water and the water may be either "warm" or "cold," depending on the machine. Often the operator can select between either a warm or cold rinse. If a warm rinse is selected, both the cold and hot water valves are opened so that about equal amounts mix and flow into the tub.

Once the rinse cycle is finished, the timer signals another spin cycle to get rid of the now soapy water which has been worked out of the clothes. Most washers go through more than one rinse cycle, and in some washers the number of rinses can be selected. Others offer a warm rinse first, followed by one or more cold rinses, or you can bypass the warm rinse altogether.

PUMPS

Most automatic washer pumps can be overhauled by using repair kits which are available from dealers or distributors of washer parts. Included in the kit is usually a new shaft and seal and both should be replaced. Sometimes the impeller has to be replaced, too, especially if it is broken or severely corroded. In some cases, the impeller and shaft do not come apart; therefore, they are replaced as a single unit. Be sure,

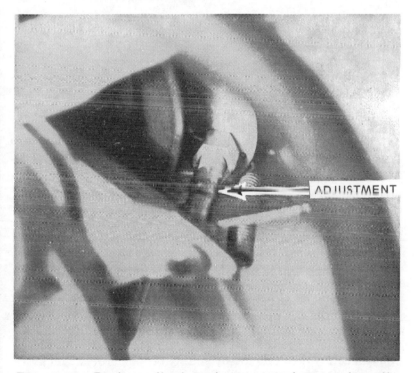

Fig. 7-12. Brake adjustment on one type automatic washer. This brake should be adjusted if the inner tub keeps spinning for a long while after the spin cycle is turned off, or if the tub is not locked in place on the wash or rinse cycles. Make sure you do not adjust the brake too tight, since it can drag on the tub during the spin cycle and cause slow spin or perhaps even damage to the drive motor or intermittent trip-out of the overload protector.

179

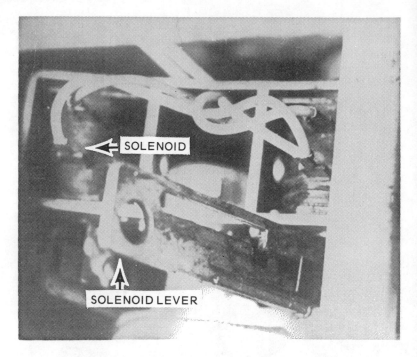

Fig. 7-13. The brake on this washer is solenoid operated.

also, to replace the gasket sandwiched between the two halves of the pump housing. When a pump leaks, it is usually around the shaft. Both the seal and the bearing may be worn out and the shaft often becomes pitted so that even a new seal will not prevent leaks.

If the pump unit is separate from the motor housing (Fig. 7-14), it is usually not too difficult to remove. If the washer is full of water (because the pump failed to pump out the water) you must drain out the water before beginning to work on the pump, otherwise you will have water everywhere (automatic washers hold a great amount of water). On some machines you can empty the machine by simply dropping the drain hose down so that the water will flow into a container or nearby drain. In other cases, you may have to disconnect a hose coming out of the bottom of the tub and squeeze it shut until you can feed it into a slightly larger hose routed to a drain or outdoors.

When removing a pump be sure to mark the position of the hoses with colored rubberbands or even a scratch mark made with a screwdriver or other sharp instrument. If the pump is belt driven, loosen the belt tightener (which may be an idler pulley) or the motor may slide back and forth in the mounting slots when the bolts are loosened.

To remove and reinstall some types of hose clamps, a special tool is required. Sometimes you can remove the clamp fairly easily with a pair of pliers but you may find it extremely difficult to replace it by the same method, especially in cramped areas. In some cases, if a tool is not available, you may want to install a different type clamp with a screwdriver adjustment.

Sometimes hoses appear to be tightly sealed to the fitting even after the hose clamp is taken off or loosened. Usually, you can grasp the hose and give it a sharp twist to break it loose. If it is stubborn, use a screwdriver or some other tool to pry between the hose and the hose fitting on the pump or tub. Fig. 7-15 shows a pump with hoses and clamps connected.

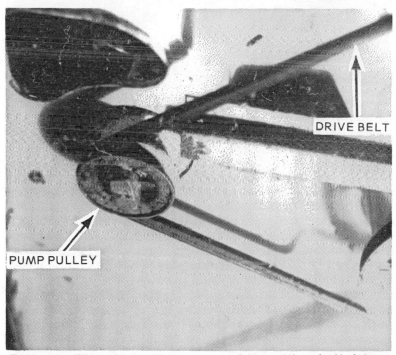

Fig. 7-14. This photo shows a machine with a belt-driven water pump. If the belt is wet, it usually is caused by a worn seal around the pump shaft which allows water to leak down the shaft on the drive belt. Although the pump may continue to function normally, the spin cycle may not work properly due to slippage caused by the wet belt.

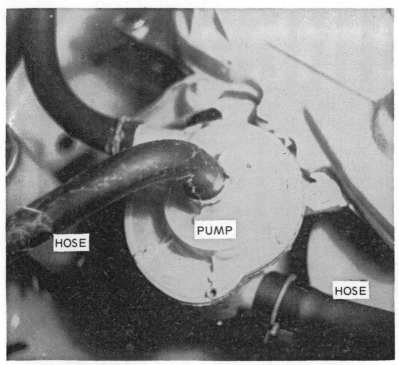

Fig. 7-15. Pump and hose connections in one popular automatic washer.

If a V-belt is used between the motor pulley and the spin transmission, it may have to be tightened if the tub refuses to spin at full speed. Nearly all washers provide some method of tightening the belt, either by moving the motor or by tightening an idler. Make sure also that there is no grease or water on the belt, since this will cause excessive slippage also. A worn belt or one that is grease soaked should be replaced.

Another thing that will keep the tub from spinning is a clogged pump or drain. If the water cannot get out of the tub, the motor will be unable to get the tub up to speed. Such an overload can burn out the motor unless it has overload protection. If the motor "clicks" off right after trying to start the spin cycle, it is no doubt overloaded for one reason or another.

If the water is not being pumped out, remove the hose running from the outer tub to the pump—make sure you have a place for the water to go—and see if the water runs out. If it does, the problem is between the pump and the drain, probably in the pump itself. If the water will not run out through the hose, probe up inside the tub; you may find that a sock or some other piece of clothing is blocking the water exit in the bottom of the tub.

Sometimes lint and other material collects around the pump shaft and causes it to bind. This will keep the machine from spinning. Lint can also collect on the impeller, in which case the pump will have to be taken apart and cleaned. If the drain hose is clogged, it could be due to an accumulation of lint or other foreign material.

TRANSMISSIONS

If you encounter trouble in a transmission you may have to remove it (most times you will), and that means removing the agitator and agitator drive block on the end of the shaft so that the shaft (which is part of the transmission) may be slipped through the housing. Since there are so many different types of transmissions and since trouble in a transmission can mean a lot of different major problems, we caution against such repairs or attempted repairs by the "Sunday afternoon" repairman. They can be repaired and parts are available for just about any brand if it is made to be repaired. There are some washers which have a sealed transmission unit; instead of repairing such units, the manufacturer recommends that they be replaced with an entire new unit. Sometimes there is an exchange program where you trade in the old one, pay the difference and get a factory rebuilt unit.

Here's one way to tell if a transmission is defective: Remove the drive belts or pulleys and release the brake or rotate the timer to the "spin" position to release the brake. Now, the inner tub should spin freely. If it is hard to turn, it's a pretty sure sign of trouble in the transmission. Caution: When making this test be sure that the machine really is in the "spin" position and that all the brakes have been released. Also, a tub full of water and clothes will be rather hard to turn.

OUT-OF-BALANCE SWITCH

Nearly all washers have a switch that will interrupt the cycle if the washer load is sufficiently unbalanced. Occasionally, the clothes accumulate or are inadvertently placed on one side of the inner tub, in which case the uneven distribution of weight causes the tub to wobble violently. The out-of-balance switch is usually tripped when the tub wobble exceeds a predetermined limit. Sometimes it can be reset with a button or the timer may have to be reset to start the cycle

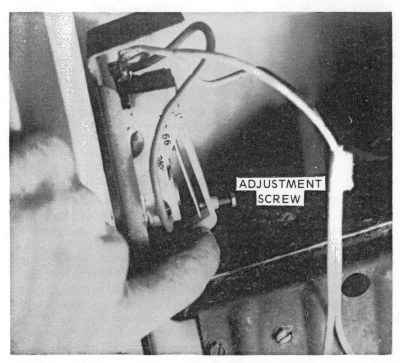

Fig. 7-16. Out-of-balance switch used in one automatic washer. It is adjusted to interrupt operation if the inner tub wobbles beyond a reasonable point.

again. Some machines automatically reset when the door is opened to rearrange the clothes into a more balanced load.

Fig. 7-16 shows one type out-of-balance switch which must be reset before the machine will start again. This switch is adjustable so that it can be set to trip when the maximum out-of-balance tolerance is exceeded. This is a factory adjustment and should not have to be reset unless the brackets are bent or a new switch is installed.

If the switch goes bad, you sometimes can sandpaper or file the points to get it going again; however, if pitting is bad, the switch should be replaced.

WATER VALVES

The water inlet valves on an automatic washer are electrically operated and are called solenoid valves. The hot and cold water valves are generally built as one unit and are referred to as water mixing valves (Fig. 7-17). These valves have screens inside to prevent foreign matter from reaching the valve itself, since a tiny grain of sand can prevent the valve from closing off the water (Fig. 7-18). When the valves start to leak (that is, allow water to keep coming into the tub during the wash cycle) it is often caused by fine bits of sediment that prevent the needle-like valve from closing properly (Figs. 7-19 and 7-20). Quite frequently this trouble will clear itself after a few more washer cycles, especially if the leak is not serious. If the leak remains, remove the water mix valve and carefully disassemble it; often all it will need is a thorough cleaning with clear water (Figs. 7-21, 7-22 and 7-23). Be sure to clean the inlet screen also and make sure that there is no silt or sediment in the valve before you reassemble it. You likely may not be able to tell what exactly was causing the leak, but unless there is obvious damage a good cleaning usually clears the trouble.

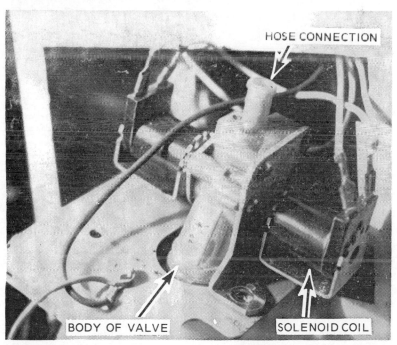

Fig. 7-17. A typical water mixing valve. Flexible rubber hoses connect from the water faucets to this valve. Usually, the "hot" water hose is marked. The hoses are especially reinforced, since under normal conditions they have water pressure on them at all times whether or not the washer is in use.

Fig. 7-18. The inlet valve connections on a typical mixer valve. Notice the screens that prevent sediment or silt from entering the valve. The screens are simply forced into each valve and can be removed for cleaning. The numbers shown on the solenoid coil (at the top) are the part numbers to use when ordering a new coil.

The water valve is pulled open when electricity is applied, so if water refuses to go through the valve, you should check to make sure that 110 volts is reaching the solenoid coil from the timer circuit. If voltage is reaching the coil, either the coil is open (check with an ohmmeter—AC power off) or the metal slug inside the valve is stuck. Another way to see if the coil is okay and receiving power is to hold a wooden or plastic stick against the side of the coil and the other end close to your ear. You should hear a hum when the power is applied (you may be able to hear it without the aid of the stick's stethoscopic effect). If the hum is heard, turn off the power and remove and clean the mixer valve as already described. Make sure the metal slug part of the valve can travel freely and is not sticking.

If the water valve does not work after cleaning carefully, it will have to be replaced. Normally, it is less trouble and often only slightly more expensive (even less expensive when you consider the time required) to replace the entire valve, with the exception of the solenoid coil, rather than attempt a component part replacement. Be sure when you remove the wires from the hot and cold water solenoids (Fig. 7-24) that you mark the wires that go to each coil. Otherwise, you could get the water valves reversed so that hot runs in when the timer is asking for cold water and vice versa (Fig. 7-25).

WATER LEVEL CONTROLS

Although some automatic washers use a "timed" cycle for filling, this method is not too satisfactory especially where

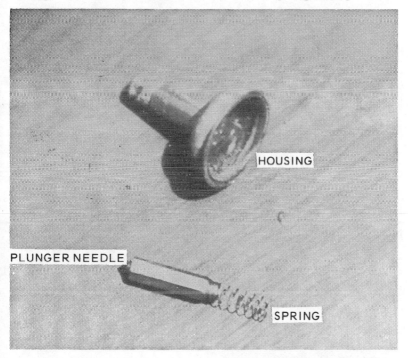

Fig. 7-19. The working parts of a water valve. The needle valve plunger is pushed down by a spring and water pressure and seats in the rubber gasket portion of the valve. Make sure that the housing, the spring, and the valve plunger are all free of dirt or corrosion. The valve plunger must be able to move freely inside the housing and have no tendency to stick.

SOLENOID COIL

Fig. 7-20. The solenoid coil has been removed from this valve.

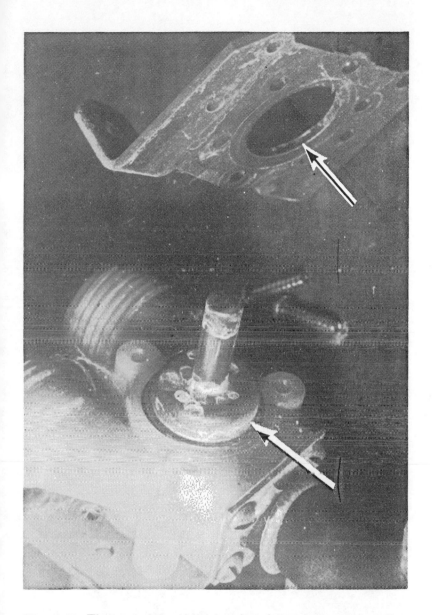

Fig. 7-21. The mounting bracket has been removed so the metal housing enclosing the needle valve can be disassembled. Take care not to tear the rubber gasket underneath the housing. This gasket is part of the valve and acts as a "seat" for the metal slug. The gasket is often sticking to the valve body and care in removing it is necessary to prevent damage to the gasket.

Fig. 7-22. The rubber valve gasket can be removed and cleaned if care is taken. Inspect the gasket carefully for any small tears or deformation at the center hole which would keep the needle valve from seating properly.

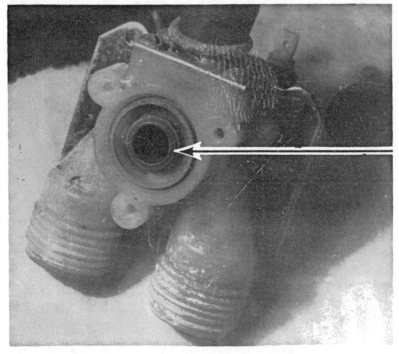

Fig. 7-23. This view shows the valve gasket in position inside the valve.

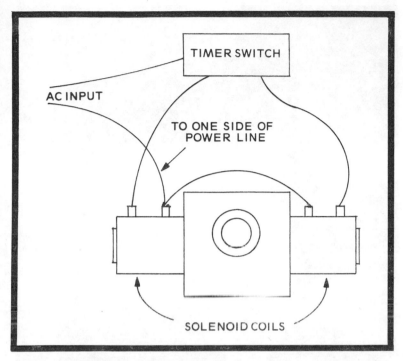

Fig. 7-24. Wiring diagram of a typical water mixing valve installation.

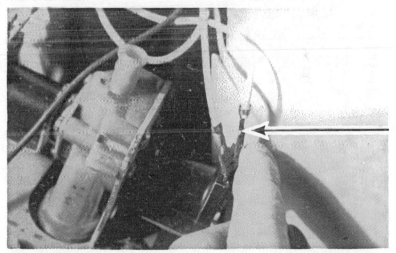

Fig. 7-25. When removing the mixing valve for cleaning, be sure to mark the wires so that you won't get the hot and cold valves operating in reverse. See Fig. 7-18.

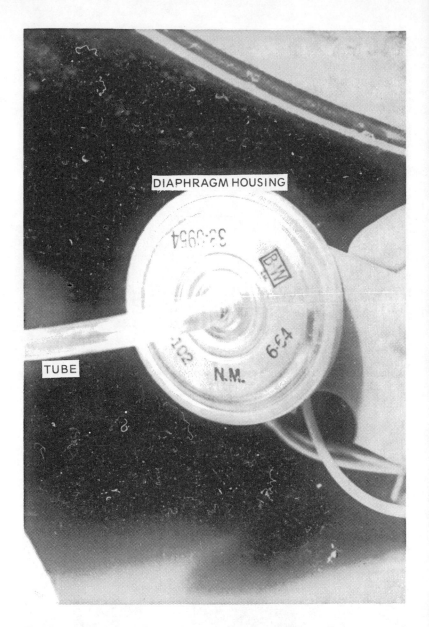

Fig. 7-26. A typical water level switch. The switch diaphragm is connected through a rubber or plastic hose to the bottom of the outer tub. When the tub fills to the correct point, the weight of the water pushes the diaphragm in far enough to activate a switch and start the timer.

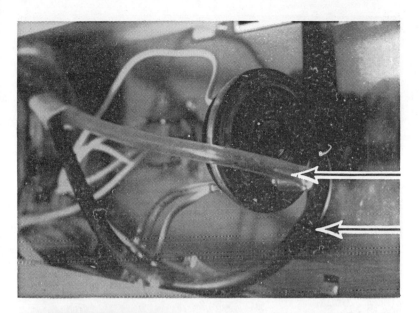

ADJUSTING SCREW

Fig. 7-27. Another view of the water level control. Notice that the tube from the control connects to a rubber boot at the bottom of the tub. The water level control generally is adjustable (if necessary) by turning an adjustment screw so as to allow more or less water in the tub before the wash cycle start.

Fig. 7-28. Two drain outlets are used on "suds saver" washers (A). The timer energizes the correct nutlet valve (B) so that sudsy water either flows down the drain or into a storage tub for reuse.

water pressure may be excessively low or high. The most popular water level control is the general type shown in Fig. 7-26. Water in the tub is allowed to flow into a small tube which is attached to one side of a sealed diaphragm. When the water level in the tub is at the correct point, sufficient pressure is applied to the diaphragm to trip a set of electrical contacts. Fig. 7-27 shows how the water level control tubing fastens into a rubber boot (or sometimes a plastic receiving tank) at the bottom of the outer stationary tub.

To test a level control, remove the wires from the switch terminals (be sure to mark them), put your ohmmeter on the R X 1 scale and check across a pair of the terminals (there will likely be three). Across one set there should be continuity, but the other set should indicate an open circuit. Now, take a short piece of tubing that fits the control and attach it to the diaphragm opening. Blow into the tubing sharply. The pair of terminals formerly showing no continuity should now indicate a closed circuit and the pair formerly closed should be open (no continuity). If you have to blow too hard into the tube to make the switch work, you may have a leak in the diaphragm or in the tubing you are using for the test. It is also a good idea to check the original tubing to make sure there are no leaks. (It is possible to have a pressure leak that will allow little or no water to leak out.) When replacing the control, be sure to get the wires back on the correct terminals.

"SUDS SAVERS"

Some machines come equipped with what has been called a "suds saver," among other names. The idea of the suds saver is exactly what the name suggests—to save sudsy water for rinse, rather than running it down the drain. When the machine finishes the wash cycle, the timer starts the washer into the spin cycle but also trips a valve to pump the sudsy water out into a container instead of to the drain. The sudsy water can then be pumped back in to wash another load of clothes. Suds saver washers have two drain outlets something like those shown in Fig. 7-28.

WASHING MACHINE TROUBLE CHART

Machine won't fill

Machine unplugged

Power off

Blown fuse

Water turned off

Solenoid water mix valve bad

Broken wire or connection to the valve solenoid

Defective timer

Sediment in the hose screen or valve

Water will not shut off

Water valve stuck open

Sediment in the water valve

Timer defective

Washer will not wash

Belt slipping

Motor not running

Broken belt

Solenoid not shifting the transmission to the "wash" position

Reset button not reset

Bad timer

Broken wire or connection

Washer will not spin

Broken belt

Belt slipping severely

Broken spring in the transmission

Solenoid clutch not working

Brake shoes not throwing out

Bearings broken or "frozen"

Timer bad

Motor not reversing (on machines using reversible motor only)

Broken wire or loose connection

Outer tub full of water

Drain stopped up or pump not working

Machine will not pump water out

Broken belt

Belt slipping

Pump binding

Obstruction in the hoses or pump

Lint in the pump or around the pump shaft

Kink in the drain hose

Drain hose clogged

Timer defective

Motor not reversing (when reversible motor is used)

Motor not running

Bad electrical connection or broken wire

Water will not stay in the tub

Drain hose too low

Broken hose

Water continues to run into the machine even when stopped

Defective water valve. Disassemble and check for sediment

Short through the timer is holding the water valve open

Chapter 8

Driers

Electric driers are basically the same, regardless of the manufacturer. All have a revolving drum mounted in a metal cabinet which opens at the front, top or back. All have V-belts or a set of nylon plastic pulleys (or both) to transfer the motor drive to the drum. An electric heating element is mounted in such a way that the heat from it is forced through the clothes as they tumble in the drum. The moisture is forced out through an air vent or sometimes down the drain. One or more thermostats control the heat at the desired temperature and prevent overheating. Safety switches normally are used to

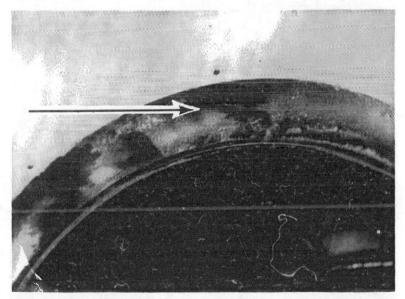

Fig. 8-1. Front of a drier with the rim and rim gasket removed to show the air passage where lint can build up if the lint trap is not doing its job. Too much lint buildup will increase the drying time and may even cause motor overload.

Fig. 8-2. Lint filter being removed from a drier door.

Fig. 8-3. Drawer-type lint filter pulled out for cleaning.

turn off the heat should the drum stop rotating for any reason. A safety switch also stops the drum when the loading door is opened.

Most driers operate on 220-volts simply because of the heavy current requirements. On 220 volts you can get the same amount of heat with only half the current flow, which means that there is much less loss in the connecting wires. (Doubling the current in a given line increases the losses by four times or, said another way, by cutting the current drain in half the line losses decrease to one-fourth.)

Usually only the heater unit is connected to 220 volts inside the drier; the motor normally operates from 110 volts. This means that the control system must deal with two voltages. Normally, only one motor is used in a drier, and it not only rotates the drum but also drives the blower that carries away moisture from the wet clothes.

Some driers have a lint catcher to prevent lint from reaching the blower fan and clogging the air passages (Fig. 8-1). The lint trap should be cleaned before operating the drier so that the air flow is not restricted. In most cases, the lint trap lifts out easily and the lint can be cleared away with the fingers. It may be located in or near the door, or there may be a separate door on the top to allow access to the trap. Fig. 8-2 shows a lint trap or filter being removed from the door. Some lint traps pull out at the bottom of the drier as the one shown in Fig. 8-3. If the lint filter has not been used or if it has a hole in, lint can build up inside the air passages until the drum rotation is impeded.

When the drier drum fails to operate, a common cause is a defective door switch, which must turn on when the door closes. Fig. 8-4A shows a door switch that has been taken loose from the drier frame for testing. Fig. 8-4B is another type of door switch. On front-loading driers, the top usually comes off fairly easily. You may need take out only a couple of screws at the rear (sometimes none at all), then use the heel of your hand to drive the top forward (or sometimes toward the back) so that it unhooks from catches in the frame. Often the switches and timer are fastened to the top, so you won't be able to completely remove it; however, in most cases you will be able to swing it up enough to make necessary inspections and tests.

The drier drum is supported by rollers at the bottom. Fig. 8-5 shows a typical drum roller. If lint builds up around these rollers they may lock and refuse to turn causing the drum to drag down or even stop and the motor may possibly overheat or even burn out.

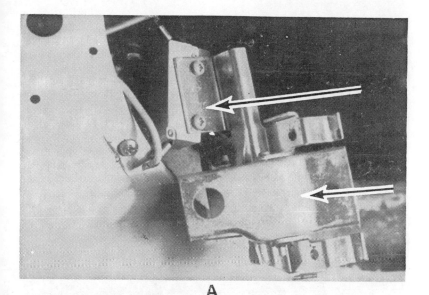

A

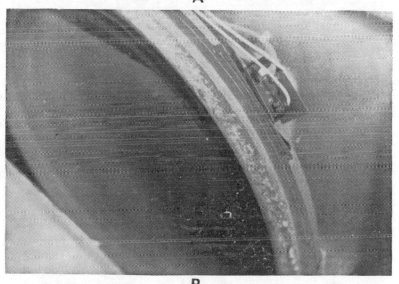

B

Fig. 8-4. Two types of door switches are used on electric driers. The type at "A" can be removed by taking out four screws. Watch that the return spring, located on the switch shaft, does not drop down into the bottom of the drier when the switch is removed. The switch at "B" is located so that the front of the drier must be removed to gain access to it.

Fig. 8-5. Rollers support the front of the drier drum. There is one on each side. Lint buildup can cause the rollers to drag. The roller bearings may also freeze due to a lack of oil. Squeaking rollers should be immediately lubricated or permanent damage will result.

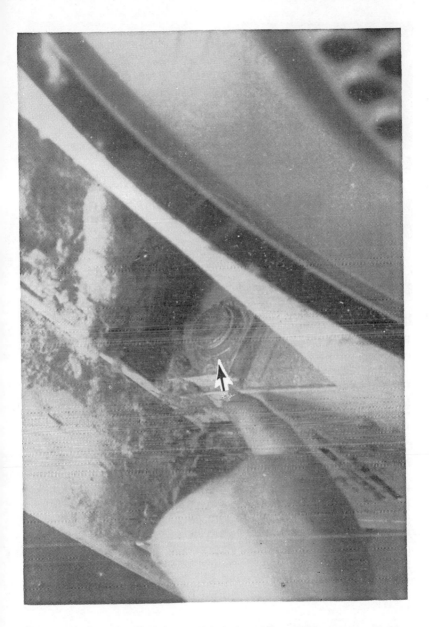

Fig. 8-6. An overload or "high heat" switch opens if the temperature inside the drier reaches a dangerous level. It will automatically close again when the drier cools down. Lint buildup inside the air passages can cause the overload switch to open because of insufficient movement of the warmed air.

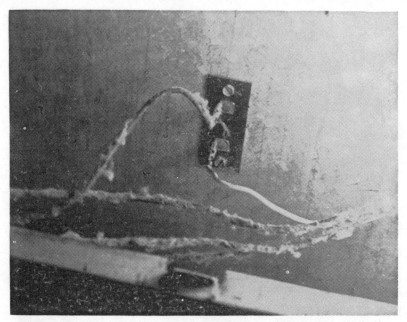

Fig. 8-7. Some driers have a fuse that extends through the housing as shown here. This is a special fuse and the top of the drier must be removed before it can be changed. The fuse wire is small and it is often difficult to tell whether it is burned out or not. The best way to check it is to disconnect the power, remove one of the leads from the fuse holder and check with an ohmmeter.

Driers employ an overload switch to shut off the heat if it rises beyond a predetermined level. Fig. 8-6 shows a disc-type thermostat that opens if the temperature inside the drum rises too high and closes when the heat returns to normal. On some driers there is a fuse, something like that shown in Fig. 8-7. This fuse can be reached only by removing the top.

Whenever a drier is disassembled for any repair, make sure to clean out the lint thoroughly, not only from the normal air passages but from around the motor, pulleys, belts, etc. This practice can prevent future trouble.

INSTALLING A DRIER

Since most driers require 220 volts, a special plug and receptacle are needed. (It is not good practice to install a drier without a plug and receptacle due to the inconvenience in servicing it, moving it for cleaning, etc.) If the nameplate indicates the drier draws 20 amperes or less, you can use a 3-12 cable from the fuse or breaker box if the run is not too long. A 3-10 cable should be used if the current drain is more than 20 amperes.

A drier plug is normally different from a 220-volt range plug because of the lower current drain, thus the larger range plug is unnecessary. Fig. 8-8 is a drawing of a typical drier receptacle. Be sure the drier is level or it may vibrate as it turns.

The vent pipe usually comes out the rear of the drier and an opening should be made through the wall of the house to allow the moisture to be discharged outside. A special trap-door type wall vent is available which automatically opens when the fan in the drier starts forcing air against it and closes again to keep out outside air when the drier is turned off. Flexible hose is used to connect between the drier and the outside vent.

ELECTRICAL TROUBLESHOOTING

A drier may appear to be completely dead and unless you are aware of the wiring used, you may not be able to quickly

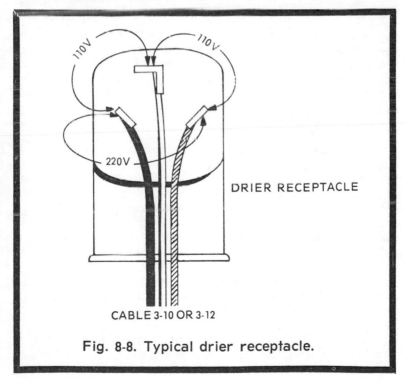

Fig. 8-8. Typical drier receptacle.

Fig. 8-9. This drier motor has a switch that turns on when the motor reaches operating speed. The switch prevents the element from heating when the motor is not running, such as when the door is opened. To check the switch, disconnect the wires from the switch and short them together with a clip-clip jumper and see if the heating element now heats.

find the trouble. If the motor is not running, you should not expect the element to heat. This is a protective feature to prevent clothes from burning up should the drum not be turning. Some driers have a switch inside the motor that closes only when the motor is nearly up to full speed (Fig. 8-9). This switch keeps the element from turning on until the motor is running. Other driers have a cam-operated switch that is on only if the drum is turning. Still others may have a switch that is turned on by the belt-tightening idler pulley between the motor and drum. If the belt breaks, the idler pulley opens the switch and turns off the heating element. Most driers have more than one safety switch to prevent the element from heating if some fault occurs.

With the belt-tightener idler pulley-operated switch, if a new belt of slightly incorrect size is installed, it could be that the pull on the switch is insufficient so that even when the drum seems to turn normally the heater element will not turn on.

There are several ways to check the electrical system in a drier. The safest way is to unplug it from the power line and make preliminary checks, at least, with an ohmmeter. Follow the input line through the various safety switches and see if they are all working. Of course, the safety switch on the motor will be open but all others should be closed. Probably the best way to check the motor switch is to use a jumper wire across the switch terminals to see if the heater element turns on when you temporarily plug in the drier for a few seconds. Or it can be checked by elimination; if all other circuit components are okay, the problem just about has to be in the motor switch. This motor switch is a fairly frequent offender, since it carries rather heavy element current.

To replace the switch, the motor has to be removed and taken apart. Loosen the motor mounting bolts and remove the belts. The blower fan is generally on one end of the motor, so after the motor is loosened, you will have to slide the motor out gently so as to not bend the fan blades. After the motor is out of the drier remove the fan from the motor shaft and disassemble the motor.

MOTOR DOESN'T RUN

A motor that does not start may not be getting power. This can be caused by a defective fuse or switch. Make sure power is getting to the motor by either measuring the voltage or by taking a plug-clip jumper and applying 110 volts AC directly to the motor input terminals. Make sure they are the input terminals and not the element switch wires!

If the motor hums but does not start, it may be due to a bad starter switch, an open starter winding, or the blades of the fan could be bent so far that they are touching some obstruction. Also, don't overlook the possibility of "frozen" motor shaft bearings due to lack of lubrication. If a motor cannot start because of a bent fan or locked bearings, the starter winding will burn out unless there is some sort of overload protection. Some types of overloads reset themselves and keep trying to start the motor at regular intervals, while others, must be manually reset. The reset button is often a small red button on the motor housing. But it is sometimes located on the timer panel.

Unlike refrigerators, the motors on driers and washing machines generally use a centrifugal starting switch that opens when the motor gets nearly up to speed. If the starter

Fig. 8-10. A typical speed reduction arrangement in a drier. The motor pulley is shown at bottom right. The large upper pulley is directly attached to the drum. The large lower pulley is not only a speed reduction unit, but it generally functions as an idler and belt tightener. By correctly applying tension on this pulley, both belts can be held tight.

switch goes bad, the motor has to be disassembled to replace it.

The motor may or may not have a starting capacitor, but if one is used, always check it for a defect if the motor hums but doesn't start. **Always make sure you disconnect the drier from the power supply completely before you start to remove parts for service. The voltages inside a drier are deadly. Be careful!**

Fig. 8-10 shows the drive arrangement in a typical drier. Notice that two reduction pulleys are used to reduce the speed of the drum to that desired. The reduction pulleys here are under spring tension so that both belts are kept tight. The pulleys themselves are usually held to the shaft with one or

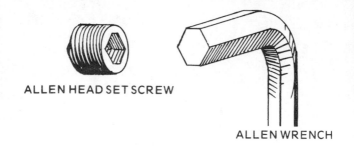

ALLEN HEAD SET SCREW

ALLEN WRENCH

Fig. 8-11. Drawing of an Allen set screw and wrench.

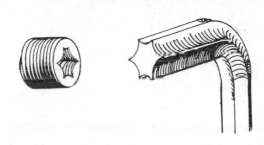

Fig. 8-12. Spline-type or Bristol set screw and wrench.

Fig. 8-13. Clutch-head set screw and wrench.

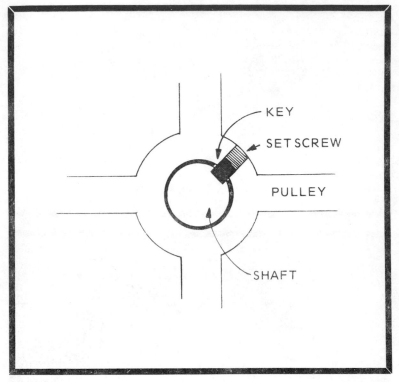

KEY

SET SCREW

PULLEY

SHAFT

Fig. 8-14. Keys are used in some cases to prevent slippage between the pulley and shaft.

more set screws, generally of the Allen type. (Allen heads have a hexagon-shaped recess that must be tightened or loosened by a matching haxagon wrench, Fig. 8-11.) In some cases, the set screws have a spline-type recess. These are called Bristol head set screws (Fig. 8-12). Also used on occasion are the clutch-head screws (Fig. 8-13). Direct driving pulleys often have a key which extends into channels cut into the pulley and shaft as shown in Figs. 8-14 and 8-15. Usually, only one set screw is required on a keyed pulley and it is placed directly over the key and slot.

Any squeaking heard in a drier should be investigated immediately and corrected with oil. The drum bearing especially needs lubrication, since it carries an uneven load, especially when clothes are wet and first placed in the drier (Fig. 8-16). Some drier drums have support rollers at the front which need oil occasionally and especially if any squeaks are noticed. Sometimes there is a felt strip around the front of the drum. It is used to support the drum when it is loaded. Occasionally the felt strip may have to be replaced. It can be reached by removing the front of the drier.

WIRING DIAGRAMS

When checking the electrical circuits of a drier, don't overlook the usefulness of a wiring diagram if one is available. Most new driers have the wiring diagram glued to the back, but this may become damaged with use. Fig. 8-17 is a photograph of a typical wiring diagram. The diagram may

Fig. 8-15. The drum drive pulley is held on the shaft by a large washer and cap bolt. Most drum drive pulleys use a slot and key to prevent the pulley from slipping. Sometimes the pulleys stick to the shaft and are difficult to remove. In such cases, a gear puller is necessary to remove the pulley from the shaft. Don't forget, though, that there may be a set screw in the pulley; be sure it is loosened before attempting to use a gear puller or the pulley may be broken.

Fig. 8-16. By removing tension on the idler pulley the belts can be easily removed. When working on a drier always be sure to lubricate the moving parts and bearings before reassembling. Some bearings have an absorbant to hold oil and these should be oiled with a good grade of motor oil of about 40 weight. For bearings without absorbing material, use a hard grease on the bearings and shafts. Here a drier repairman is shown removing the bolts from the brackets that holds the idler pulley to the housing. Bracket should be marked so you will know how to replace it.

reveal a hidden switch or overload protector that needs checking before jumping to an incorrect diagnosis. A good way to use the wiring diagram is to start at one of the "hot" power line terminals and follow each line using an ohmmeter to determine if each of the components in the circuit has continuity. Again, remember that some switches have continuity only when the motor is running or the drum is turning.

You can also use the wiring diagram to determine how you can "jumper out" a particular switch or circuit to ascertain whether or not it is operating. For example, is the motor switch suspect as the reason for the heating element not turning on? Use a jumper across the switch and check by temporarily turning on the drier. If the heater element turns on, the switch is suspect. Or perhaps a heat limit thermostat has developed a permanent open; again, you can jumper across the thermostat and plug in the drier for a short interval to see if the heater element turns on again.

Fig. 8-18 shows the heater element or "burner" used in one model drier. Other and later driers use Calrod type enclosed elements which must be replaced as a unit if they go bad. On the type shown in Fig. 8-18, the element wire can be replaced, or it is possible to repair a break in this type of heater element if the wire is not too old and brittle. If it is broken near a terminal, simply stretch the wire to the terminal and place it under the nut or screw. For breaks farther out, where removing a part of the wire might shorten it so much that it would draw too much current, use a short bolt with two heavy metal washers and a nut and wrap the broken ends around the bolt and tighten the nut. You must make sure that the bolt cannot come in contact with the drier frame (and don't forget that the element wire will expand and sag when heated).

Twisting the wires together is normally not satisfactory, since the joint will develop a high resistance and overheat, and

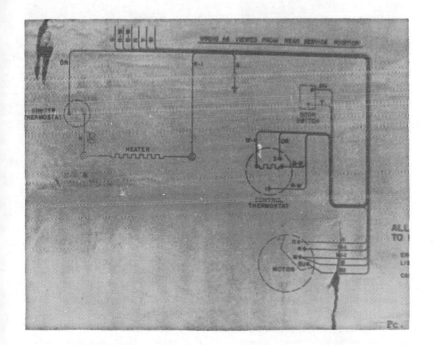

Fig. 8-17. Typical drier wiring diagram.

215

Fig. 8-18. An open, coiled-type heater element as used in some driers. This element wire can be purchased by the foot. To order you should know the wattage rating and wire size. The element wire comes in a closewound coil and has to be stretched to the proper length. The entire element should be stretched at one time. Run a string through the insulators from one terminal to the other, then remove the string and measure it. Stretch the coil of wire by pulling on each end until it reaches the length of the string, then thread through the insulators and connect to the line terminals.

burn open again at or near the same point. The bolt and washers not only make a low-resistance splice but the metal carries away heat from the splice, making it less apt to give future problems.

Fig. 8-19 is an enclosed element with three leads. One half of this element may open and the drier will appear to be working; however, it will be slow in drying clothes.

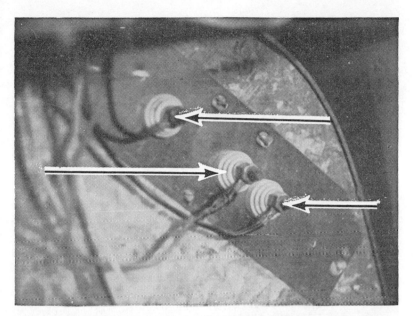

Fig. 8-19. This drier has a heating element with three terminals.

Fig. 8-20. Back view of a typical timer.

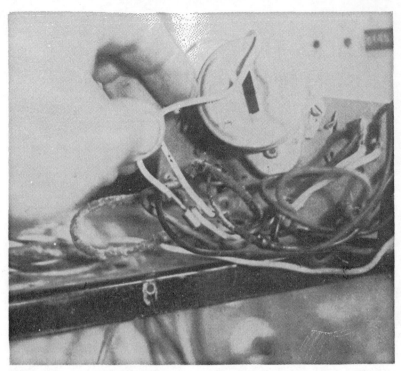

Fig. 8-21. Leads to the timer motor can be checked with an ohmmeter to see if there is continuity. Or you can use a plug-clip jumper connected to the motor windings to see if the motor runs. **Be sure** that the drier power plug is pulled when either of these tests are made.

TIMERS

Drier timers are essentially of the same sort as those found on other appliances. Some are simple with only three or four wires, since they are used only for turning the drier off and on. These simple types turn the motor on, let it run for a specific length of time, then switch it off. Fig. 8-20 is a view of the back side of a drier timer.

Timers can be checked by removing the wires coming from the terminal blocks. An ohmmeter will tell you whether or not the motor winding is good (Fig. 8-21) and if the switch is turning off and on as required.

Most timers operate on 110 volts, but a few may operate on 220 volts. Timer switches usually control only a 110-volt circuit, turning the motor on; the internal motor safety switch switches on the element. In the exceptions to the above, the timer switches a 220-volt circuit or perhaps two 110-volt circuits.

DOOR SWITCHES

Door switches are necessary so that when the door is opened, the drier drum will stop, thus preventing potential injury and the possibility of clothes being spilled out on the floor. A rather frequent trouble in driers is a defective door switch. You can check the door switch by removing it from its mounting and connecting a clip-clip jumper across the switch to see if the drum will turn. Or you can check the switch with an ohmmeter, but be sure to disconnect the power first. Remember that the switch is off when released and on when pushed in. The door switch is often a 2-way switch, in that it turns off the motor when the door opens and turns on a light that shines into the drier drum; see Fig. 8-22.

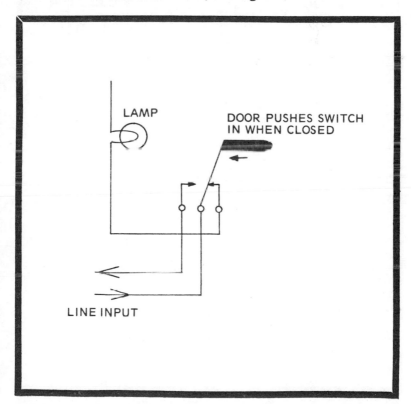

Fig. 8-22. Door switch circuit which also controls a drum lamp.

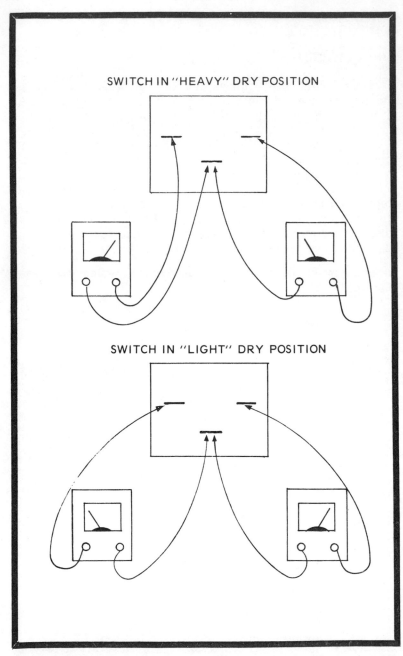

SWITCH IN "HEAVY" DRY POSITION

SWITCH IN "LIGHT" DRY POSITION

Fig. 8-23. An ohmmeter can be used to check a temperature selector switch.

TEMPERATURE SELECTOR SWITCH

The temperature selector switch generally has three or more terminals. For "heavy" drying, the switch connects 220 volts to the drier element; for "light" drying the element may be connected to 110 volts. Also, there is usually a "no heat" position which is used for "fluffing" clothes which are already dry. After removing the connecting wires (be sure you mark the wires so you can get them back on the switch correctly) check between the terminals as you rotate or flip the switch. Two of the switch terminals should be connected in all positions except the "no heat" or "off" position. Two terminals should be connected for heavy and another two for light drying. Fig. 8-23 shows how the ohmmeter might read, depending on the position of the switch.

Fig. 8-24. This thermostat is located just above and to the side of the drier drum. After one lead has been removed from the circuit, the thermostat can be checked with an ohmmeter.

THERMOSTATS

Thermostats are "go-no go" devices; that is, they are either on or off. When a thermostat is used for determining temperature, it is controlled by on-off action; for higher temperatures the thermostat is on more and off less. Regardless of the thermostat type, you can check it for correct operation with an ohmmeter. Just be sure the power plug to the drier is disconnected and be sure that all leads are disconnected from one side of the thermostat so you won't get a false continuity reading. Fig. 8-24 is a control thermostat, and Fig. 8-25 is an "overheat" thermostat.

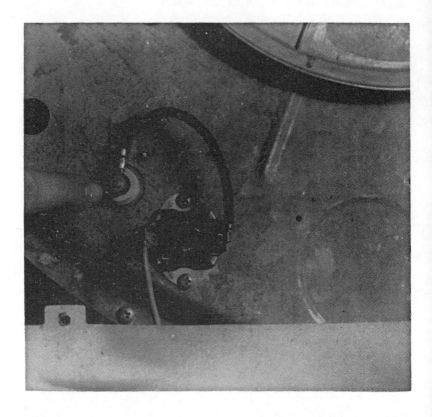

Fig. 8-25. This is an "overheat" thermostat which disconnects the heater element if the drum temperature exceeds a certain level.

DRIER TROUBLESHOOTING
Motor runs but the heater element will not come on

Element switch inside the motor is defective

Element is defective

Fuse or breaker open in 220-volt house circuit

Thermostat or temperature control switch is defective

Loose wire going to the heater element

Lint buildup in the screen or lint trap

Drier improperly connect to the power line.

Fan not moving enough air

Too much lint buildup in the lint trap or in air passages

Outside vent is clogged

Loose fan blade

Motor running too slow

Too large a load in the drier

Drum running too fast

Motor inadvertently connected to 220 volts instead of 110.

Belts placed on pulleys incorrectly

Incorrect replacement motor used on the drier.

Clothes take too long to dry

Fabric switch is set wrong

Wires on the wrong terminals of the switch

Clothes too wet when placed in the drier

Part of the heater element burnt out

Loose wire to the element terminal

Flow of air restricted by lint

Loose fan on the motor shaft

Too large a load of clothes

Thermostat shutting off too quickly

Dial on the temperature switch slipping

Drier gets too hot

Thermostat going bad

Lint holding heat-limit thermostat is open or preventing it from sensing heat.

If thermostat has a heat-sensing bulb it may be located incorrectly.

Lint buildup in the drum or air passages

Fan not moving enough air

Too much lint in lint trap filter

Drum will not turn

Motor is not turning

Belts are broken or slipping

Idler pulley spring is broken or loose

Drum bearing is frozen

Idler pulley bearing is frozen

Pulley is loose on the motor or drive shafts

Lint between the drum and the drier frame or housing

Rollers that support the front of the drum are frozen

Motor will not run

Check fuse at the fuse box (or breaker)

Motor bearing is frozen

Heavy lint on the fan blades

Drum bearing or idler pulley shaft bearing is stuck

Starter switch inside the motor is defective

Door switch is defective

Fuse inside the drier (when used) is open

Motor capacitor is open

Motor windings are burned out

Chapter 9

Water Heaters

Basically, there are two types of water heaters: the belted type and the submerged element type. In belted types the heater unit does not touch the water but wraps around the metal tank instead, heating the tank, which in turn heats the water inside. Fig. 9-1 illustrates the general location of the belts. The elements may be the "Calrod" type or they may be open elements mounted in insulating and heatproof blocks. To replace the element in a belted type heater, you should tie the new element onto one end of the defective element, then pull out the old element while feeding the new one in its place.

In the submersible element type (Fig. 9-2), the element is inside the water heater tank, submerged in the water. A submersible element may be attached to the tank, through a hole in the side of the tank, by four bolts; some elements screw into the side of the tank. To remove the screw-in type, first disconnect the electrical wires, then use a large wrench or socket to unscrew the element by turning it counterclockwise.

For elements that are mounted with bolts, it is necessary to pry them loose from the tank after removing the bolts since they probably will be "stuck" to the tank by the rubber gasket seal between the heating element and the tank. Lime and mineral deposits may make the old element hard to remove so that you will have to turn the element back and forth several times, gradually forcing it out of the tank. Obviously, before removing a submersible element the water tank needs to be drained and the water intake closed off.

Submersible elements come in different shapes and sizes. The replacement obviously must be of the same general type as the original with mounting flanges to match. There are also different electrical wattage ratings. Check the nameplate on the heater to determine the correct size. Most of the time there are two elements in the water tank, one at the bottom and the other at the top. The two elements may have different wattage ratings; for example, the nameplate may indicate a 1000-watt element at the top and a 1500-watt element at the bottom, or they may have identical wattage ratings. Each of the elements

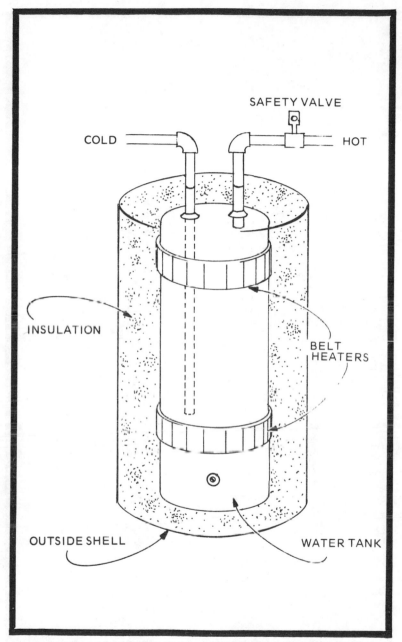

Fig. 9-1. Drawing of a belted-type water heater. The insulation in belted types is always considerably thicker than in submersible element types.

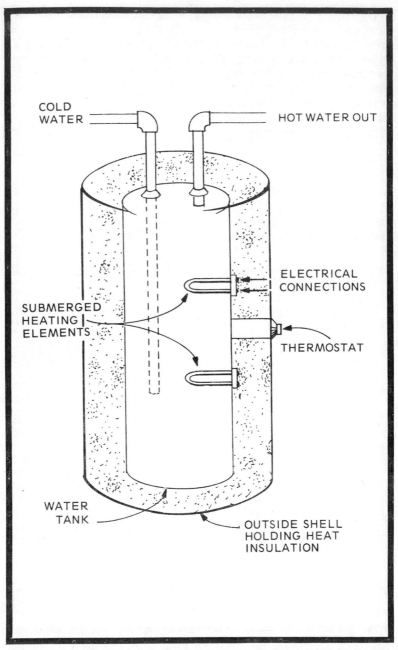

COLD WATER

HOT WATER OUT

ELECTRICAL CONNECTIONS

SUBMERGED HEATING ELEMENTS

THERMOSTAT

WATER TANK

OUTSIDE SHELL HOLDING HEAT INSULATION

Fig. 9-2. Drawing of a water heater with submersible elements.

is controlled by thermostats. Normally, the top element heats first and when it kicks off the lower element turns on. This is true whether the elements are the belt type or the submersible type. Some water heaters are called "quick recovery" heaters. The only difference is in the wattage rating of the elements. Quick recovery units have considerably higher wattage ratings, especially on the top element. Fig. 9-3 is a picture of a submersible element as it looks mounted in the side of the water tank.

INSTALLING A WATER TANK

The fuse or circuitbreaker used with a water heater depends upon the amperage rating of the heater. The amperage rating may not be on the nameplate; usually, there's only a wattage rating. To determine the amperage from the

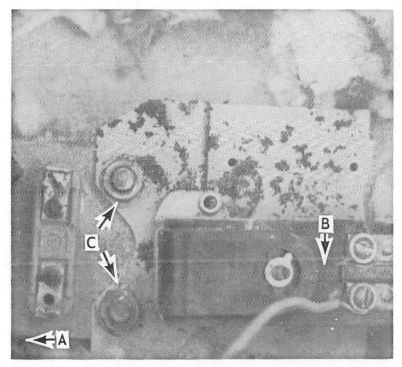

Fig. 9-3. Submersible element mounted in a tank. The letter A indicates the bolts that hold the element in place. The thermostat (B) controls the temperature of the water, and C points to the electrical terminals.

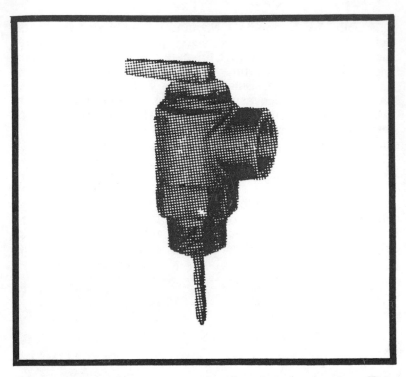

Fig. 9-4. Typical pressure valve for a water heater. This Pfister valve is made from red brass with a stainless steel spring and silicone washer. It is available in pressure ranges from 50 to 200 PSI and it automatically reseats itself.

wattage rating, divide the line voltage used into the wattage. For example, if the rating is 2200 watts and the line voltage used is 220 volts, the amperage rating would be 2200 divided by 220 or 10 amperes, or should the combined wattage rating be 3300 watts, the combined amperage drain would be 3300 divided by 220 or 15 amperes. When wiring the heater, however, it may be incorrect to calculate the amperage from the total wattage rating, since only one element will be on at a time in most cases. In this case, to calculate amperage rating, use the wattage rating of the largest rating element. For example, if one element is rated at 3300 watts and another at 4400 watts, calculate the amperage for fusing and wiring by the 4400-watt rating only, meaning that the maximum current drawn by the heater at any one time will be 4400 divided by 220 or 20 amperes.

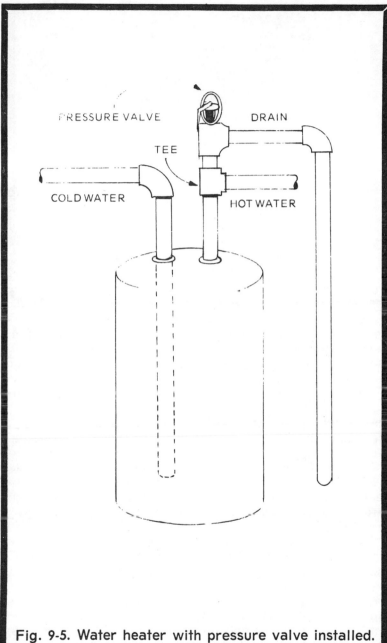

PRESSURE VALVE

DRAIN

TEE

COLD WATER

HOT WATER

Fig. 9-5. Water heater with pressure valve installed.

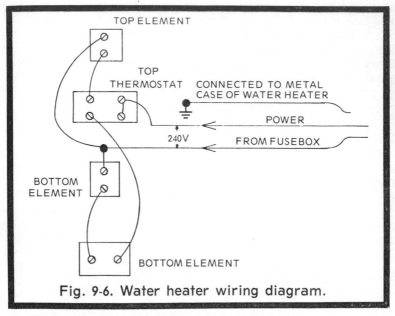

Fig. 9-6. Water heater wiring diagram.

Water heaters which draw less than 20 amperes can be wired with 3-12 wire (3-wire cable with size 12 wire). For heaters drawing more, use 3-10 wire. Be sure that the water heater is grounded by the third wire to the fuse box to prevent the possibility of electrical shock.

A safety valve should be installed on the hot water line to prevent the possibility of excessive pressure buildup should a thermostat fail. If a thermostat fails and heats continuously, the water will boil and create excessive pressure inside the tank. Without the "pop off" valve, if a thermostat sticks the water tank will burst with such force as to cause considerable property damage as well as possible personal injury to those nearby even though they may not be in the same room. The safety valve should be piped to a drain (Fig. 9-5) or connected to a line outside the room where the water heater is installed.

A junction box on the back of the heater is provided for the electrical connections. There should be four wires in the box—two from each element. Fig. 9-6 shows a typical wiring diagram for a 2-element water heater. Notice that the current for the lower element and thermostat must pass through the upper thermostat. This is so the lower element cannot turn on until the upper element has turned off. Since hot water rises to the top of the tank, the upper element provides quick recovery because it does not have to heat all the water in the tank to provide hot water to the output pipe. Fig. 9-7 shows an upper thermostat installation; notice that it has four terminals, two of which are connected together to form a common terminal.

The upper thermostat is a single-pole double-throw switch (SPDT) while the lower thermostat is a single-pole single-throw (SPST). If the mounting is the same, an upper thermostat may be used to replace a lower thermostat by using only the normally closed terminals (usually the top two or the two on the right where all the screws are in line).

SERVICING A WATER HEATER

Before looking for trouble inside a water heater, make sure that power is available. Check the fuses or cir-

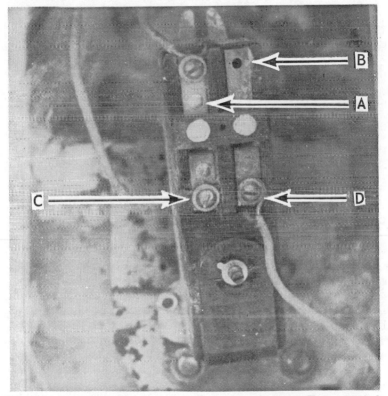

Fig. 9-7. Upper thermostat in a water heater. Terminal A connects to one side of the power line and one thermostat terminal; Terminal B goes to the other side of the thermostat. The power line connects to Terminal C (same as A). When the thermostat opens, Terminal C is connected to D and supplies the bottom thermostat.

Fig. 9-8. This panel conceals the thermostats and element connections in this water heater.

cuitbreakers. Next, remove the panels necessary to gain access to the thermostat and elements. Fig. 9-8 shows the panel to remove on one make water heater.

You can check a heater element with an ohmmeter. Remove the lead from one element terminal and check across the element with the ohmmeter on the R X 1 scale. If the meter reads half scale or so, it is a good indication that the element is okay. You can also use a test light; see Fig. 9-9.

Another way to check is with an AC voltmeter. Turn up the thermostat and check to see if there is 220 volts (plus or minus about 5 percent or so) across the element. This test should be made before any wires are removed from the element. **But be careful when making this test: Do not touch the bare terminals because 220 volts is lethal, and do not touch one lead and the metal case of the heater since there will be 110 volts between the terminals and the case and 110 volts can kill also!**

Another precaution: **Remember that water heaters are often located in damp areas and you can receive a killing shock if you touch one side of 220 volts while standing on a damp floor, especially a concrete floor. Make sure that the test leads on your voltmeter are well insulated and, as an added precaution when working on hot circuits, wear rubber-covered gloves.**

Fig. 9-10 shows one type of thermostat used with a belted-type heater element. For emergency repairs, you can bypass an element and thermostat. If, say, the top element is burned out, the bottom element cannot work because the top thermostat will never turn off and supply voltage through the other set of terminals to the lower thermostat. The simplest way to

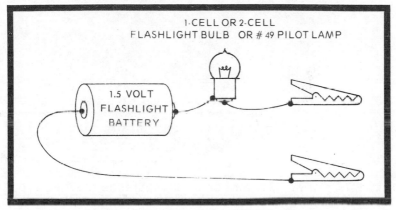

1-CELL OR 2-CELL
FLASHLIGHT BULB OR # 49 PILOT LAMP

1.5 VOLT FLASHLIGHT BATTERY

Fig. 9-9. A simple continuity tester you can build. Tape the lamp to the side of the battery after making the connections. Touching the two clips together will light the lamp. To check continuity of a thermostat switch, for example, connect the clips across the switch terminals then heat the thermostat. (If light turns off you know that switch is working.) The light should light when the thermostat is below the setting on the dial. Remember that in all continuity testing you should turn **off** all external power to the water heater. It is also a good idea to take off all the wires from one terminal on the item to be tested so that you don't get a false indication. In water heaters you should always check between one of the element terminals and the metal shell of the water heater with a continuity tester, if the light lights, the heater element is shorted and must be replaced. To check for shorted elements it is better to use an ohmmeter on the R X 100 scale and if there is any meter reading the element should be replaced.

235

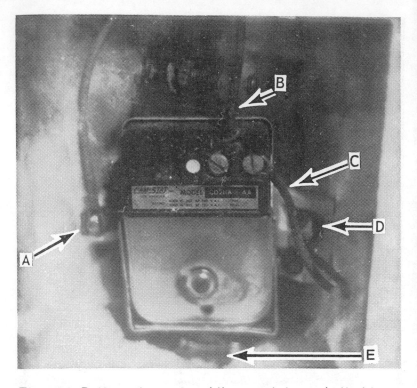

Fig. 9-10. Bottom element and thermostat on a belted-type water heater. "A" is one terminal of the bottom heater element, which returns to one side of the 220-volt power line. "B" is the line coming from the top thermostat. "C" is the line from the thermostat to the other side of the bottom heater element, Terminal "D". "E" indicates the clamping bolts which hold the belt element tight around the water tank. The bottom element in this heater is the same as the top element and the thermostats are the same, except the top thermostat has two extra terminals for turning on the power to the bottom thermostat when the top thermostat kicks off.

temporarily correct this trouble is to place a shorting wire across the two thermostat terminals which switch on the lower element, as shown in Fig. 9-11. If the top thermostat is defective, remove one lead from the top element and connect a jumper wire so that voltage will be applied to the bottom element through the bottom thermostat. The heater will be slow to recover heavy hot water usage, but it will work nor-

236

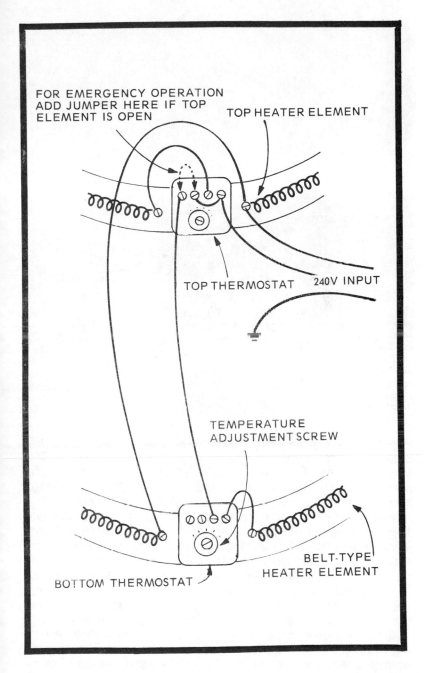

Fig. 9-11. Wiring diagram of a typical belted-type water heater.

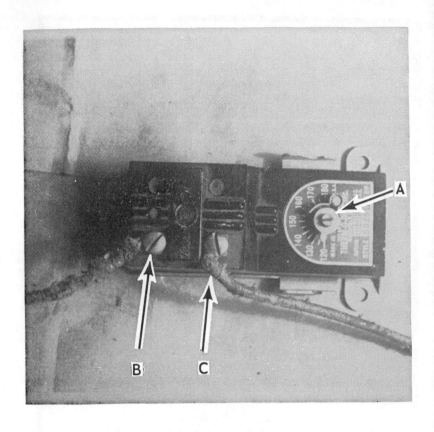

Fig. 9-12. A simple type thermostat used on some water heaters. "A" is the temperature-adjusting screw. "B" and "C" are the thermostat switch terminals which control the current to the heater element. To check the thermostat, remove one wire from the electrical terminals. Connect an ohmmeter (R X 1) scale across Terminals B and C. Use a soldering iron or match to heat the thermostat on the back side (Fig. 9-13). As soon as the thermostat heats up, the ohmmeter should indicate that the switch has closed. Note: Ohmmeter should read zero ohms. If the meter reads any resistance, it is likely that the thermostat points are pitted severely and the entire thermostat will have to be replaced. Make sure to zero your ohmmeter before testing by shorting the leads together and setting the "zero adjust" until the meter pointer reads exactly zero. "Zero" on most ohmmeters is at full-scale with the pointer to the extreme right edge of the meter scale.

mally otherwise. Water heaters with a burned-out lower element or thermostat will continue to supply hot water but not nearly in so much abundance, though recovery time may be as quick as ever.

One of the big disadvantages with submersible heating elements is the lime buildup, which reduces the efficiency of the heating element and eventually forces it to be replaced. Fig. 9-14 shows an element which had to be replaced because of excessive lime buildup. Belt-type heaters, though more expensive when purchased, generally last much longer because lime and mineral deposits inside the tank are virtually nonexistent, except under extreme conditions.

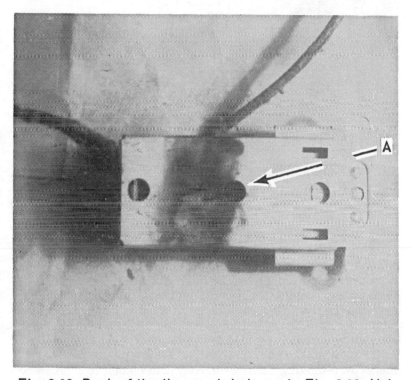

Fig. 9-13. Back of the thermostat shown in Fig. 9-12. Hole at "A" is to allow heat to reach the bimetal strip inside which activates the switch contacts. Bimetal strips warp when subjected to heat and so can be used to move switch contacts. The front adjustment on the thermostat moves the bimetal strip closer or farther away from the contact points so that the thermostat will turn off on a lower or higher temperature, depending upon the dial setting.

Fig. 9-14. This submersible element had to be replaced because of the lime buildup.

If a heater element shorts it can run up the electric bill without causing an overload sufficient to blow a fuse or multibreaker. This is why the leads should be removed from the element (both leads) during servicing, and a check made between the terminals and the metal frame of the heater with either a test light or ohmmeter. Any leakage between the element and frame means that the element must be bypassed. In the case of a bottom element, an emergency repair can be made by removing both leads from the element; tape (electrical tape) the ends of the two leads (apart) so they cannot short against the frame of the water heater. If it is the top element that is shorted, remove the leads from it and tape them, then rewire the circuit so that the input power leads go directly to the lower element and thermostat. Make sure that the connections are made correctly; otherwise, the thermostat can be ruined! Fig. 9-15 shows a wiring diagram with the top element and thermostat bypassed.

WATER HEATER TROUBLE CHART

Heater won't heat

Fuse is blown

Broken wire

Loose connection; check the screw terminals

Thermostat is open; to check, temporarily connect a jumper across the terminals, then turn on the power and see if the element heats, or check with an ohmmeter or test light

Top element is open; check with an ohmmeter or test light. Reset button (when used) is tripped out; reset. Heater is connected to 110 volts instead of 220 volts

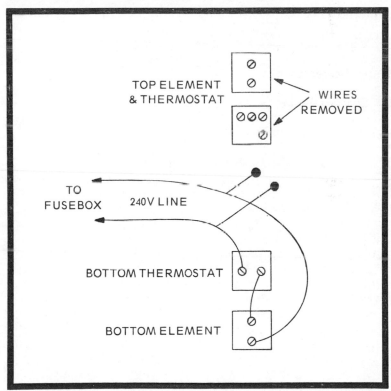

Fig. 9-15. Wiring diagram showing the top element bypassed.

Water not hot enough

Thermostat(s) is set too low

Bottom thermostat is defective

Bottom element is open

Bottom element is shorted

Water too hot

Thermostat(s) is set too high

Thermostat(s) is sticking in closed position

Thermostat(s) is improperly connected

Slow recovery

Top element may have been bypassed previously

Water heater shocks

Shorted element

Broken ground wire

Thermostat shorting through

Broken insulation on lead wire, allowing a short to the metal frame of the heater

Chapter 10

Garbage Disposers

Although there are a number of different makes of garbage disposers on the market, all work essentially the same way Some are larger and have more powerful motors; thus, there is less chance that they'll hang up. Bones—especially chicken bones—are probably the most frequent cause of disposer hangup, since they sliver and wedge in the hammers or between the hammers and the frame.

MOUNTING

The disposer is normally located on the bottom side of a two-basin sink with its opening attached to the drain opening. Fig. 10-1A shows the bottom side of the flange that is inserted through the hole in the sink. Some models have a rubber gasket that goes between the sink and the flange on the

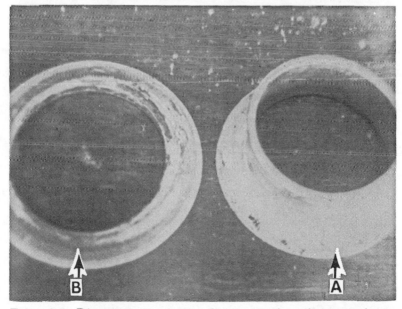

Fig. 10-1. Disposer mounting flange and sealing washer.

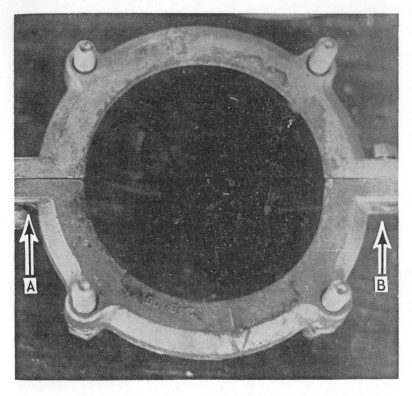

Fig. 10-2. Ring used to clamp to the flange that mounts to the sink.

disposer. Sometimes a caulking compound is used instead of a rubber gasket. Fig. 10-1B is the washer that fits up against the bottom of the sink. The washer is installed after the flange is put through the sink. Again you should have a rubber gasket or caulking compound to apply before the washer is put into place.

Fig. 10-2 is the ring which clamps to the flange that fits through the sink. A and B are the two screws that hold the two parts of the ring together. The flange on the lower part of the sink has a flare or ring on the bottom of it so that when the ring is in position and tightened, it will not slip off the bottom of the flange. The ring secures the flange and washer to the sink and prevents leaking. Fig. 10-3 shows how the ring looks after it is taken apart, ready to fit in position on the flange. The ring must be placed in a certain way. The bottom has a groove for a gasket that fits on the disposer. One of the adjustment screws

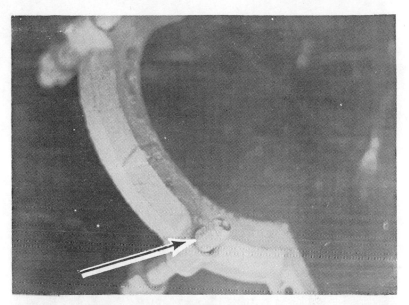

Fig. 10-3. The arrow indicates one of the adjustment screws used to tighten the ring, washer and flange in the bottom of the sink.

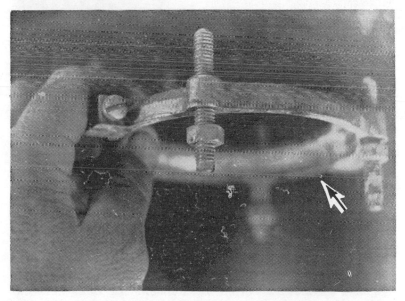

Fig. 10-4. In this view of the clamp ring, you can see the groove that seals against a gasket on top of the disposer unit.

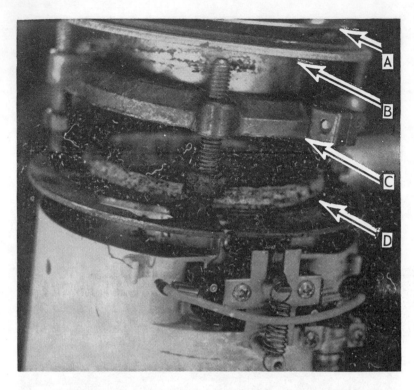

Fig. 10-5. This disposer is suspended from the nuts on the clamp ring adjustment bolts. The flange on the disposer is pushed up over the nuts and turned slightly counterclockwise. Then the nuts are tightened.

used to secure and tighten the ring, washer and flange in the bottom of the sink is indicated by the arrow in Fig. 10-3. The arrow in Fig. 10-4 is pointing to the groove in the ring which accepts a gasket that effects a seal between the disposer and ring.

The top part of the garbage disposer assembly is shown in Fig. 10-5. Flange A is inserted through the sink drain opening. Washer B fits around the underside perimeter of the sink drain opening and prevents water from leaking. The ring (C) clamps around the lower flange on the lower side after it is inserted through the sink. When the ring is tightened washer B is sealed against the bottom of the sink. The flange or connection plate on the disposer (Fig. 10-5D) hangs on the nuts extending from ring C. Slotted holes in the flange (D) allow the disposer uniti to be pushed up until the adjustment nuts extend through the holes; then a ¼ turn locks the unit in position. When the nuts are tightened, the disposer top is sealed to the clamp ring. The sealing gasket is shown in position in Fig. 10-6. The slotted mounting holes in the flange are more evident in Fig. 10-6. As you can see, one end of each slot is big enough to allow the mounting nuts to pass through.

SWITCHING

Disposers are normally turned on manually, either with a separate toggle switch or sometimes by turning a cap at the drain opening. Some disposers have a rubber lid which is placed over the drain opening to prevent waste from splashing out while the unit runs; others have a rubber diaphragm with slits cut in it so the waste can be pushed down through. The slits close when the waste has been pushed through. The

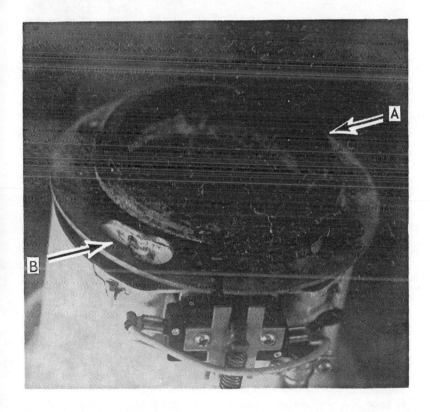

Fig. 10-6. A rubber gasket is used to seal between the disposer and the ring clamp.

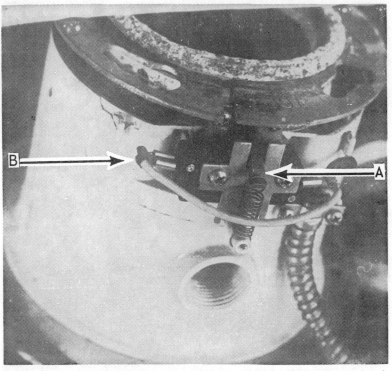

Fig. 10-7. Disposer switch location (A), and line terminal (B).

typical garbage disposer shown in these photos has an internal switch which is activated by turning a seal cap at the drain ¼ turn. Other disposers may use a separate external switch to turn the disposer off and on.

The switch in Fig. 10-7 is indicated by arrow A. A finger that extends down inside the disposer operates the switch. When the top is in place and turned to the proper position, the switch finger is pushed down and turns the disposer on. Fig. 10-7B is one of the terminals where the line connects to the switch. To check the switch, remove the leads and connect an ohmmeter to the switch terminals. When the switch finger is pushed down there should be continuity through the switch. If there is no continuity, the switch is bad and will have to be replaced. The switch can be checked with the power on if care is taken. A screwdriver can be used to locate the finger of the switch on the inside of the disposer. After it has been located, push down on it. If the disposer runs the switch is good, of course. However, if the switch finger is bent, it may not be coming into contact with the plunger on the top of the disposer unit. The switch finger could be broken off or worn out. It is possible to repair a switch finger, but it has to be put back in the proper position.

Plunger-operated switches can be replaced with a toggle switch mounted in a convenient location. The old switch itself will have to be left on, though, because without it a hole will be left in the side of the disposer and water can leak out. A replacement switch is simply connected to the wires removed from the old switch.

DRAIN CONNECTION

The normal trap and drain is fastened to the outlet side of the disposer. Anything passing out of the drain is ground into

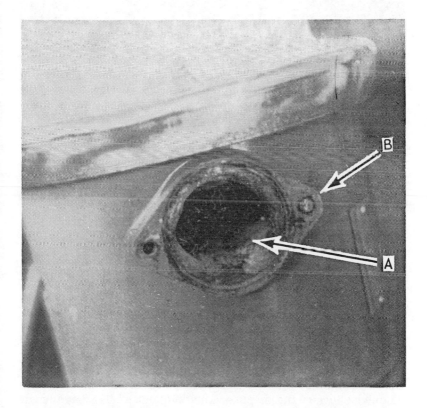

Fig. 10-8. Disposer drain connection. After aging, the mounting studs are prone to twisting off (B).

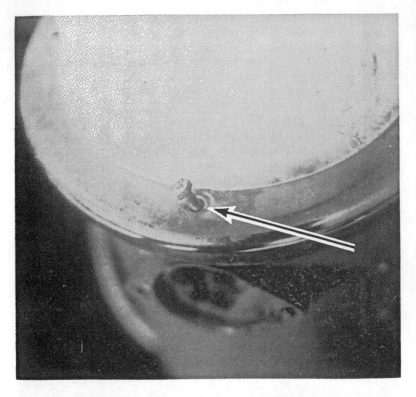

Fig. 10-9. The disposer unit itself is held together by studs.

small pieces by a set of hammers or blades. The pieces are ground fine enough so that they will pass through a screen with small holes in it. Water must be run into the disposer as it grinds so the waste will be flushed down the drain. Housewives should always be cautioned to use plenty of water so that the waste material will not "blob" up and clog the drain.

The location of the connection between the sink drain and the disposer is indicated by A in Fig. 10-8. Before the disposer can be serviced the drain has to be disconnected. Care should be taken when loosening the studs (Fig. 10-8B) in the drain connection flange or they may twist off, in which case they will have to be drilled out and removed before new ones can be installed. After the drain has been disconnected, the mounting nuts at the top of the disposer can be loosened. Then a slight clockwise turn of the disposer should release it. If it is turned before loosening the nuts, the rubber gasket could be damaged and require replacement.

Fig. 10-10. With the studs removed, the top of the disposer can be lifted off.

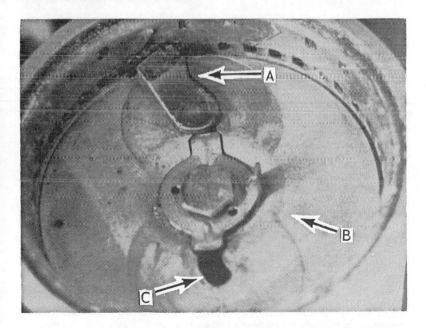

Fig. 10-11. Top view of the disposer grinding mechanism.

251

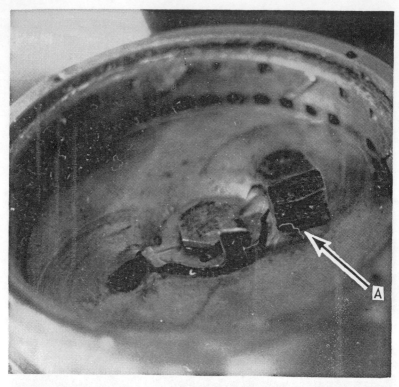

Fig. 10-12. The grinding hammer is shown in the backward position.

SERVICING

The disposer unit itself is held together by studs (Fig. 10-9) which are inserted through the top flange and screw into a flange or the base. Obviously, the disposer can be taken apart by removing the studs (Fig. 10-10). In Fig. 10-11 you can see the bottom half of the disposer after the top half has been removed. The hammer or beater (A) swings in or out; it swivels and changes positions to allow seeds and other materials that get caught between the hammer and the wall to fall away. If the hammer lodges it can cause the turntable or metal disc (B) to bind and stop the motor. The second hammer in Fig. 10-11 has been removed to show the slot into which it fits (C).

Fig. 10-12 shows the grinding hammer in the backward position, which demonstrates the clearance available between the hammers and the screen or knives. After wastes are

Fig. 10-13. When waste particles are small enough, they pass through the holes indicated.

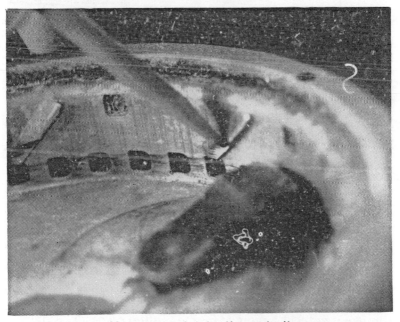

Fig. 10-14. Knives assist in the grinding process.

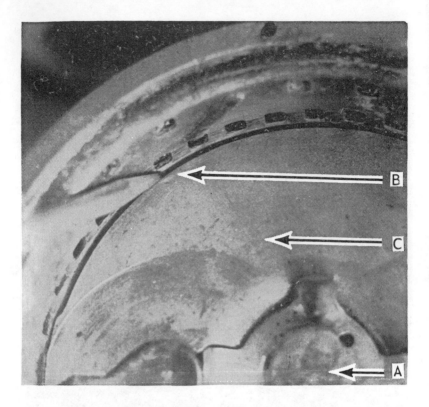

Fig. 10-15. Objects that lodge in the narrow space between the disc and side of the disposer can lock the unit.

ground fine enough, they pass through the holes indicated in Fig. 10-13. Sometimes the holes fill up, in which case they will have to be cleaned with a wire brush or an old toothbrush. Knives, indicated in Fig. 10-14, help cut up waste as it is thrown against the sides of the disposer.

The disc or spin table (Fig. 10-15C) can be lifted out by removing the stud (A). The space between the disc and side of the disposer (B) is just large enough to allow objects to lodge and stop the disposer. Hair pins, needles, hulls, paper clips, etc. can fall in this small crack and cause trouble. Such lodging usually occurs when the disposer shuts off or just before it stops spinning. When this happens the spin table or disc cannot move and the disposer simply will not start the next time it is turned on.

Sometimes you can see the object causing the bind and remove it without having to dismantle the disposer. Extreme

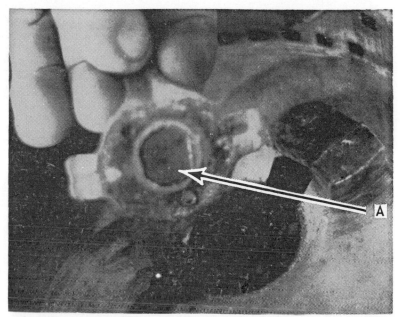

Fig. 10-16. Stud and washer which hold the hammers in place.

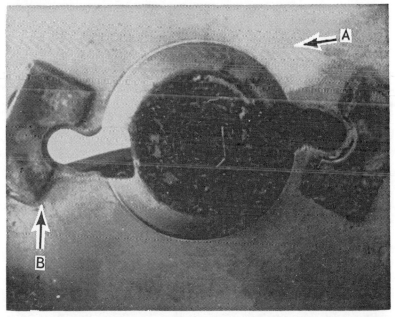

Fig. 10-17. Disc or spin table removed from the disposer.

Fig. 10-18. A knob or flare on the hammers holds them to the disc or spin table.

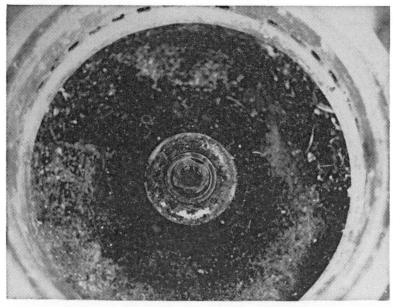

Fig. 10-19. The bottom area in the disposer, where waste particles fall, must be cleaned out occasionally.

care should be taken to make certain the power to the disposer has been turned off before starting to work on it. If the power is still on and the switch is one that is turned on from inside the dispenser, the switch could be touched accidentally. If pliers or a screwdriver happens to be down in the disposer extensive damage could result. Or even worse, if a finger, instead of a screwdriver, were down in the disposer, a severe injury could occur.

In Fig. 10-16 a repairman has removed the stud and washer (a type of lock washer) which hold the hammers in place. Now, the disc or spin table (Fig. 10-17A) can be lifted out. A re-enforcement plate (B) helps hold the hammers secure and keeps them from wearing through the spin table. Hammers are held to the disc by a flare or knob on the end of the shaft (Fig. 10-18). After waste is chopped fine enough, it drops to the bottom of the disposer (Fig. 10-19) where it is

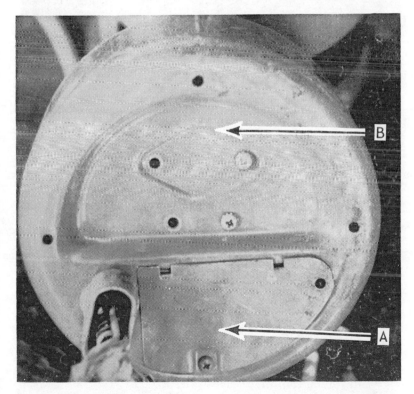

Fig. 10-20. View of the bottom cap. The power connections are concealed behind plate A and the overload behind B. The power line is just visible at the lower left.

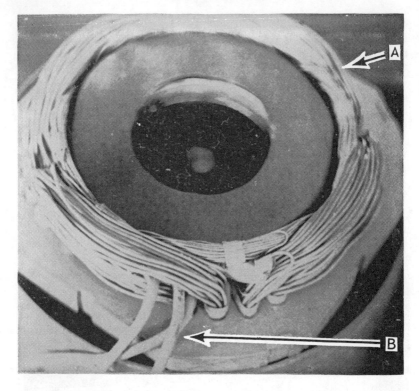

Fig. 10-21. The motor windings (A) are visible with the bottom plate removed. The wire leads (B) go to the relay and overload.

flushed down the drain. Sometimes this area must be cleaned out so the disposer will work properly.

Electrical

The power connections are located behind plate A in Fig. 10-20, along with the relay or motor starter switch. The entire bottom can be taken off by removing two screws from around the sides. Plate B (Fig. 10-20) is removed to gain access to the motor overload protector. In many disposers the overload switch button is located on the side near the bottom and is accessible without removing any plates.

With the bottom plate removed (Fig. 10-21), you can see the motor windings (A) and the leads coming from the relay and overload (B). Fig. 10-22 is a view of the inside of the bottom plate. The motor relay that disconnects the start winding

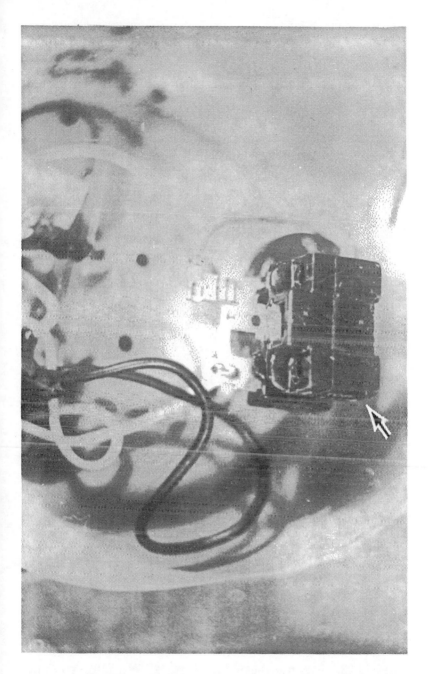

Fig. 10-22. Inside view of the bottom cover with the motor starting relay indicated.

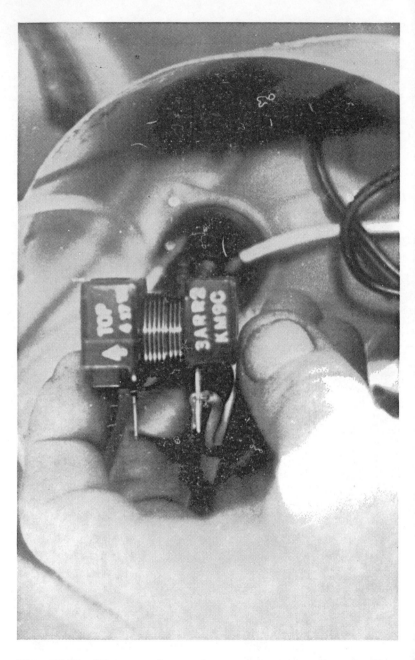

Fig. 10-23. The numbers stamped on a motor-starting switch and the horsepower rating are necessary to order a replacement.

after the motor has reached three-quarters running speed is visible. The relay position is critical; therefore, it must be mounted a certain way. The relay should be marked with an arrow—this side up—on top. If the motor is not running properly, the relay could be the trouble, especially if the motor checks all right. The best way to check the relay is to replace it with a new one. If it works, the old relay obviously was the source of the trouble. The motor terminals can be removed and the relay checked with an ohmmeter as discussed earlier. It is important to mark the leads so they can be replaced properly. All relays should have identifying numbers stamped on the side of the unit, as shown in Fig. 10-23. To order a replacement, the motor horsepower and relay number are needed.

The motor overload is shown in Fig. 10-24. If the disposer clogs or if the motor should become overloaded for any reason the device opens and stays open until reset. An ohmmeter can be used to check it by removing one wire from one terminal of

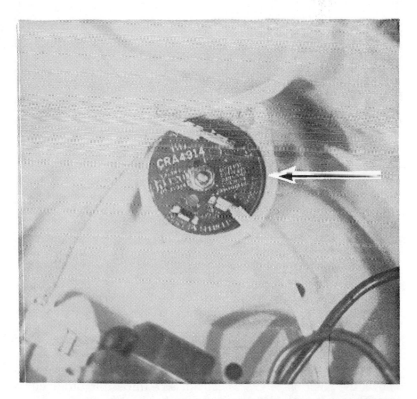

Fig. 10-24. Overload protector in a typical disposer.

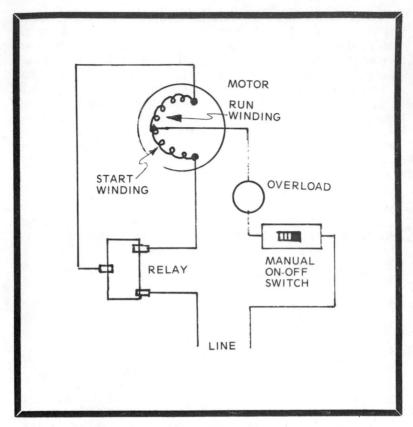

Fig. 10-25. Wiring diagram of a typical disposer unit.

the overload. The ohmmeter leads are simply connected across the terminals of the overload. If there is no meter reading, the overload is bad and needs to be replaced. The overload could be bad and still show continuity, but usually the bimetal disc in the overload will be burned up and there will not be a reading. The overload element is a bimetal strip or disc that opens the circuit when heated to a certain temperature. As a result, if the motor is pulling too much current or is binding, the resulting increase in current will heat the overload. Occasionally, if an overload protector is heated almost to the point of opening, it may lose its efficiency and thus create problems, all the while appearing to be okay when checked with an ohmmeter. The wiring diagram in Fig. 10-25 shows the position of the overload, as well as the other components, in a typical disposer circuit.

DISPOSER TROUBLESHOOTING CHART

Disposer won't run

    Blown fuse

    Disposer unplugged

    Bad switch

    Loose connection

    Bad overload in the motor

    Motor burnt up

Disposer tries to run but can't

    Foreign material between the spin table and housing

    Loose hammer

    Bad overload

    Relay bad

    Starting capacitor bad

    Low voltage

    Bearing frozen

    Buildup of material under the spin table

    Disposer loaded too heavy

    Start or run windings in the motor are burnt out

Disposer starts but doesn't run

    Relay bad

    Overload bad

    Low voltage

    Spin table binding

Bearing is stuck or frozen

Drain clogged up

Not enough water to carry the food down the drain

Disposer is not grinding food

Hammers are out of place

Spin table is not turning

Loose on shaft

Motor not getting up to speed

Relay bad

Low voltage

Ports stopped up along the sides

Not enough water

Buildup under the spin table

Drain is clogged

Disposer throwing food out the top

Cap not in place

Rubber missing in the mouth of the disposer

Seal bad between the sink and disposer

Disposer leaking

Loose nut on the drain

Seals between the sink and flange are bad

Loose flange and washer in the sink

Broken studs in the flare connection on the disposer

Chapter 11

Ranges

Electric ranges are nearly always wired into a 220-volt separately fused AC circuit. For obvious reasons this is called a "range" circuit. Range circuits usually are fused with 50 or 60 ampere fuses. Since the circuit is 220 volts, there are two fuses in the range box, one for each of the hot lines. Ranges are wired with 3-wire cable and normally a 3-wire range plug is provided for disconnection when necessary. The three wires are the 220-volt mains and a ground wire. From each side of the 220-volt lines to ground you should measure 110 volts. The clock or oven light, if used, is operated from one of the 110-volt

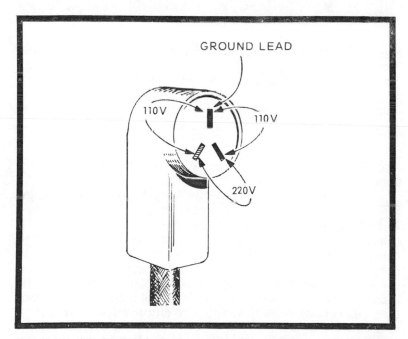

Fig. 11-1. Typical range receptacle, called a "crowfoot" type.

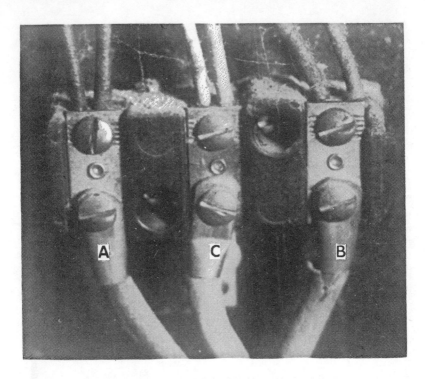

Fig. 11-2. Somewhere on the back of an electric range there will be terminals for attaching the 3-wire line cord. Terminals A and B are the "hot" leads and C is the ground. If you were checking voltage, there should be 220 volts AC between Terminals A and B and 110 between Terminals A and C and between B and C.

circuits. Most ranges also have a convenience outlet for plugging in a coffee maker or some other appliance.

The wire running from a fuse box to an electric range should be 3-10 at least, and larger if the run is a long one (over 20 feet or so). An electric range plug and receptacle are usually the "crowfoot" type shown in Fig. 11-1. The range cord, with the male plug to fit the crowfoot receptacle, is normally 36 to 42 inches long. It may have to be purchased separately when a new range is bought. It has three pigtail leads with eyelet terminals which is connected to the three terminal screws located somewhere on the back of the range (Fig. 11-2).

One of the pigtail leads or terminals on the cord is usually a different tone or color to indicate it is the ground terminal.

The other two may be connected as desired, since it makes no difference whether they are reversed or not, but the ground terminal must go to the ground terminal. The ground terminal on the range is nearly always the center terminal. Another fairly accurate indication of the ground lead is the color white; in electrical wiring, a wire with white insulation is or should be a ground wire. The term "ground" wire does not indicate that the wire goes to earth ground, though in actual fact it will return to earth ground through the power line system, but rather it means a "common" circuit.

Fig. 10-3 shows the 3-wire system used in distributing electrical power. If lamp L1 and lamp L2 were the same size, there would be no current flow in the ground or common circuit since the two lamps would be lit in series across the 220-volt circuit. However, if one lamp is larger than the other, the larger lamp will require the most current and this extra

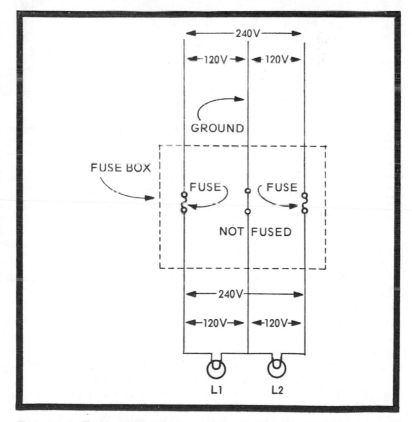

Fig. 11-3. This sketch represents the 3-wire systems used in all house wiring.

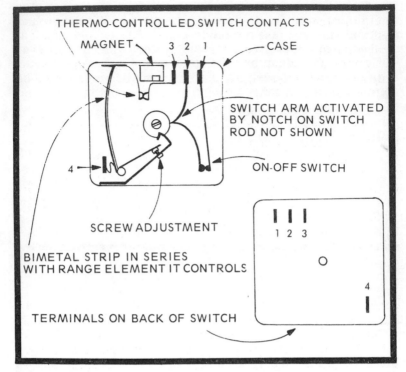

Fig. 11-4. Inside and rear view sketches of a "continuous" range switch.

current has to travel through the third or ground wire. If lamp L1 draws 2 amperes, for example, and lamp L2 draws 3 amperes, the ground wire will carry 1 ampere.

RANGE WIRING

Obviously, the internal wiring of ranges will differ from one to another, depending upon the complexity of the control circuits, especially. The simplest ranges may only have the four burner switches and a thermostatically controlled oven switch. The most expensive ranges may (and usually do) have clock controlled ovens and sometimes surface (top) burners. The oven is thermostatically controlled, along with perhaps one or more of the burners. The surface burners may be step controlled; that is, they may have burner switches with from four to seven or more positions, or they may be continuously variable between very low heat and maximum heat.

The oven switch and thermostat are generally one unit, but the switch will have a sensing device on a tube somewhere inside the oven so that the oven temperature is automatically controlled at the desired setting. The oven normally has two elements—one on top and the other at the bottom. Either or both may be turned on, depending on the setting of the oven switch and thermostat.

The various step-controlled burner heating arrangements usually apply either 110 or 220 volts to the burner and the burner elements are connected either one at a time, in series, or in parallel. On modern ranges, however, it has become a common practice to use a "continuous" switch which may or may not have detents to give it a "click-click" action. Fig. 11-4 shows the internal action of one of these switches, some of which are even more elaborate. Essentially what happens is that when the switch knob is rotated it turns the switch shaft and the cam fastened to it. The cam has a notch into which the off-on switch arm falls in the "off" position. When the switch knob is turned clockwise the arm is forced out of the notch and the switch contacts close. With the bimetal strip cool, the contacts fastened to it are also closed so current flows to the element or burner. If the switch is moved up only slightly past off, there is not much tension on the bimetal strip so it does not take too much current to heat it sufficiently to pull the contacts apart and open the burner circuit. But with the contacts open there is no current through the bimetal strip so the strip cools and presently allows the points to spring back together and complete the circuit again, starting the process over. As the knob is advanced clockwise, more tension is placed on the bimetal strip to hold the contacts closed; therefore, more heat is required before the contacts open. As a result, the burner gets hotter.

The magnet used in the switch gives a "snap action" to the contacts and minimizes arcing when the points open or close. The magnet holds the points closed until a certain tension on the bimetal strip can pull the points apart. The magnet has the most pull when the contact arm is directly against it, so when the arm starts to pull away the magnet suddenly releases all its hold and the arm springs away quickly, opening the points.

A few ranges are equipped with a thermostatic sensor (Fig. 11-5) at the burner which senses the amount of heat and turns the burner off and on, depending on the position of the switch. When this type of thermostat goes bad, it is best to replace both the burner switch and the thermostat, otherwise operation may be erratic.

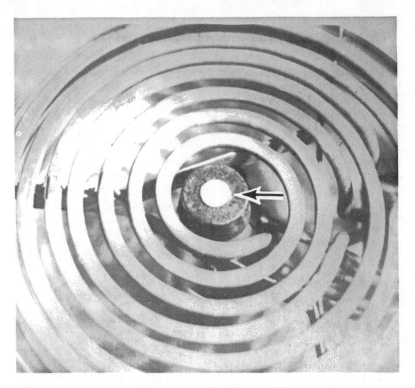

Fig. 11-5. Some surface burners have a heat sensor located in the center of the unit. The desired heat is selected with panel control.

CHECKING BURNERS

Until fairly recently all range burners were "wired in," and even though they could be removed for cleaning, as in Fig. 11-6, they were still "captive" because of the connecting wires. One of the common troubles with this kind of burner is that the wires break near the terminal points. To repair, unplug the stove from the power line, then cut off a short piece of the connecting wire and discard it. Strip off the insulation from the remaining lead end and reinstall under the terminal screws. You should do this with all the connecting leads while you are making this repair since another will likely break soon. Fig. 11-7 shows a screw terminal type burner tilted up for checking and repair.

You can check the burner for continuity with an ohmmeter if you remove the lead wire from the terminal you want to check. Often the burner will have two separate elements with a connecting bar between the common terminals of the elements. The separate elements make it possible to change burner heat by connecting only one or both of the elements to either 110 volts or to 220 volts, depending upon the position of the burner switch.

Many later model ranges use 2-terminal elements that plug into a burner socket and which are controlled by bimetal operated switches such as the one in Fig. 11-4. With the bimetal control there is no need for a tapped burner element since the heat is regulated by the length of on-off cycles rather than by the amount of voltage applied to the element continuously. Plug-in type burners cause little trouble with broken leads, since the lead wires do not move when the burner is removed for cleaning. It is a good idea, though, to make sure that the connection between the burner and the plug is solid. Any sloppiness in the connection can lead to a

Fig. 11-6. A surface burner is removed by lifting it at the front and pulling out. Some burners are held in place by a screw located in the back. Of course, the screw must be removed to allow the burner to slip out.

Fig. 11-7. View of the surface unit terminals. As you can see two terminals are connected together and the ground is connected to this terminal (A). When the switch is in a certain position, the element is connected to a 110-volt circuit. The two hot wires are connected to the other two terminals (B). These wires frequently break or burn off. Every time the burner is cleaned, the wires bend and eventually break off. To repair the connection, strip the wire end of its insulation and connect it to the screw. To check the burner, remove one hot line and, using an ohmmeter, place one lead on the terminal where you removed the wire and the other lead on the other hot terminal. The ohmmeter should give you a reading. If it doesn't, the element is bad and will have to be changed. This check measures both elements at the same time. If you use the other lead, both elements will have to be checked because you are only checking one at a time.

Fig. 11-8. A coiled type element is used in some of the older model range ovens. This type can be replaced by restringing the wire through the insulators. The wire is a special type which can be bought at an appliance or electric shop. All you need is to have a piece of the wire to determine the original physical size. The wattage rating will be found on the nameplate of the electric range. When you get the wire it will look like a spring and you will have to stretch it enough to fill the insulators where it belongs, being careful not to stretch it to the point where it isn't tight after you finish. If the element sags and touches the metal any where, it will short out and blow a fuse. The element will stretch some after it gets hot, which is normal.

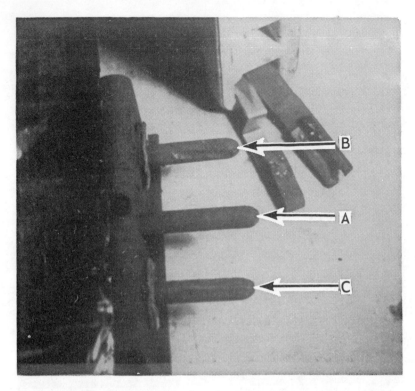

Fig. 11-9. Oven element plug-in connections are prone to corrosion and pitting due to arcing. The element is Terminal A; B and C are the 220-volt terminals.

loose connection that will cause the plug to deteriorate rapidly and soon fail to make a secure connection. Any discoloration of the plug is sufficient evidence that the connection is poor and should be cleaned and tightened.

OVEN ELEMENTS

On older ranges you may find an oven element like the one shown in Fig. 11-8, but this type has not been installed in new ranges for many years. It used to be a rather common practice to use plugs and sockets for the oven burner elements so that the element could be removed for cleaning, checking or repair. One disadvantage of this is the rather prevalent tendency for both the plug and the socket to develop "pock marks" and a glaze, preventing a solid connection, and a true rule of electrical circuits is that any electrical connection that is not "good" will heat up and aggravate the situation even more, due to arcing or burning at the terminals.

When such ranges were new, both the plugs and sockets had a shiny surface and so made a good connection, but if the connection gets loose, the shiny surface will disappear by burning or corroding away (Fig. 11-9). The plug-in connectors on oven elements are even more susceptible to this problem than other plugs since they are not only subjected to the heat generated in the oven but because the electrical current is high and heat is generated in an electrical circuit in direct proportion to the square of the current (I^2R). In other words there is four times as much heat developed across any

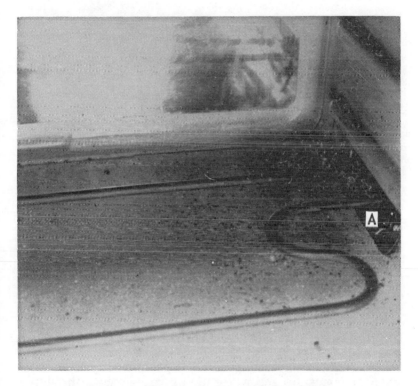

Fig. 11-10. Chromalox oven element which can be removed by loosening two screws (A). After these screws have been removed, the element can be taken out. There are two wires connected to the back side of the element. When loosening these screws, the terminal should be held with a pair of pliers so you won't break the connections off of the element. After a long period of use the screws may rust due to heat from the element.

Fig. 11-11. Like the element in Fig. 11-10, this broiler element is held in place by two screws (A). Also, top elements are supported by clips or screws. The temperature sensor (B) is visible here.

resistance in the circuit every time the current is just doubled. This means that any resistance in a connecting plug produces heat, but especially so if the current flow is high as it is in an electric range. All modern ranges use some sort of enclosed element (Fig. 11-10), such as the "Calrod" unit, and it has become almost universal practice to permanently connect the oven elements by screw terminals rather than through a socket and plug arrangements, though the latter is still used by at least two or three manufacturers on some range models.

An oven element can be checked with an ohmmeter, generally, though it is possible that an ohmmeter check may show continuity but the element will not heat, or at least not heat properly when connected to a source of power. A not too common fault, but one that happens often enough to mention, is a shorted "Calrod" unit in which the inner element shorts to the grounded metal enclosure. In some ranges, when this happens, the oven element literally burns up, much on the order of a 4th of July sparkler, even with the oven switch turned off. If this happens, and a range fuse or breaker does not blow, the range should be pulled out from the wall and the power plug disconnected. The oven element will have to be replaced; there is no repair for a Calrod or similar type unit.

The upper element in most ovens is called the "broil" element (Fig. 11-11) and is turned on only when the oven switch is in the "broil" position. Generally, only the lower element is turned on at other positions of the oven switch.

Fig. 11-12. There are almost as many types of range control panels and timers as there are models of ranges. In this case, separate dials are used for the start-stop oven functions. Notice that one button says "Push for Manual." If this button is pulled out, the oven cannot be turned on unless the "start" button is past the time indicated by the clock.

TIMERS

Range timers are basically similar to those found on driers, washers, etc. The range timer, though, usually is the most elaborate, since it nearly always has a clock that can be set to turn the oven on and off at preselected times (Fig. 11-12). Note: One of the most common causes of "oven failure" is an incorrect setting of the oven timer switch. Make sure, when the complaint is, "oven doesn't heat," that the timer settings are carefully checked. Some timers also control one or more of the top burners, though not too many ranges have this feature.

Since the timer is so complex, as a rule, the best way to troubleshoot is to first make sure the settings are correct, then carefully check other trouble possibilities before assuming that the timer is defective. By checking the wiring diagram you can usually tell which leads on the timer can be "jumpered" to see whether or not the timer switches are functioning. If the clock motor does not run, check the field coil with an ohmmeter (be sure power is disconnected). If the coil is bad, in most cases you will likely have to replace the entire timer, though a few timer clocks do have replaceable field coils. You will have to make a judgment on the spot. If other parts of the timer appear to be worn or connections appear to have been overheated, the best bet is to replace the entire timer, rather than trying to patch up an old one.

BUILT-IN RANGES

In new or remodeled kitchens you often find a built-in range, with the surface burners in one location and the oven in another. Built-in units work much the same as any electric range, of course, except for the separation of the burners from the oven unit. The separate units may have leads long enough to reach the switch box, but often the wires run to a junction box and an entrance type cable goes from the junction box to the main switch box. This wire should be at least 10 gauge or larger, and especially so if the wire run is longer than a few feet.

If either of the range units does not work, you should first check to make sure that the correct power line voltage is available, then make certain that any timers used are properly set for the action expected. Don't overlook the fact that lights on a stove that work properly do not necessarily mean that the power circuits are okay; for example, one fuse or breaker in the 220-volt circuit could be open and there could still be 110 volts available for operating the lights, timer, etc.

Also check the ground wire (usually a white wire) for proper connection. Failure to get the ground wire connected correctly can cause all sorts of odd troubles and may even cause damage to the stove or its control switches. Make sure that the ground wire goes to the ground connection on the stove and not to one of the "hot" terminals. Generally the ground wire will be the center connection of the three input terminals but don't be too sure—some will have an end terminal as ground.

TROUBLESHOOTING

Fig. 11-13 shows the wiring diagram for one type of electric range. A diagram is usually found on the back of the stove. Generally, the wires are color-coded so they are easy to follow. Range wiring uses a special kind (asbestos covered) of insulation for protection from heat. Such insulation is a little

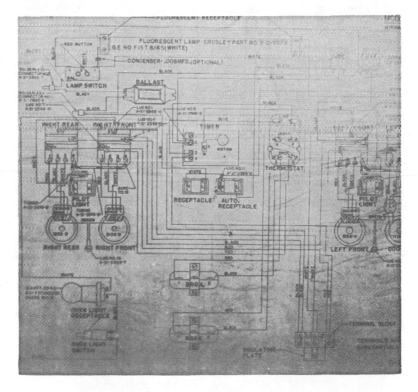

Fig. 11-13. Typical range wiring diagram.

Fig. 11-14. In some ranges, the oven light, receptacle, timer, and other 110-volt devices are protected by fuses in the range.

hard to remove and the wire should be scraped so it will make good contact with the terminal. If you have a loose wire, the connection will overheat, causing the wire to melt off, or it may keep the element from coming on or heating up like it should. The wire may even burn off and cause trouble. Sometimes slip-on connections are used instead of screws. If this is the case, you may have to get new ones to replace the originals.

Fig. 11-14 shows the location of fuses that are sometimes used in an electric range. Quite often the oven lights, the receptacle on the top of the range and the timer motor are fused. Fuses are located on the top of the stove or down next to the floor. You may have to remove a panel to find them.

ELECTRIC RANGE TROUBLE CHART

Clock will not work

    Fuse on the range is blown

    Coil is out or open on clock motor

    Broken wire or loose connection

    Motor gear is stuck

    Motor gear is stripped off

    Loose ground wire

Burner will not heat

    Wire is burnt off

    Loose wire

    Element is shorted out

    Wire is burnt in two inside the element

    Fuse is blown

    Range is connected to the circuit incorrectly

    Loose ground wire or wire is connected in the receptacle improperly

    Switch is not making contact

    Switch is bad

    Automatic switch in the "off" position

Oven will not heat

    Oven timer is in the "off" position

    Wire is loose on the oven element

    Bad oven thermostat

Element is burnt out

Element is shorted

Wire is connected to the thermostat improperly

Line wires are connected to the range improperly

Element connection is bad where it plugs into the range

Light will not burn

Fuse on the range is blown

Ground wire is loose

Bulb is burnt out

Bad switch

Wire is loose or burnt off

Oven light switch is bad

Wire is burnt off of the light switch

Range shocks

Wire is burnt off and touching metal

Element is shorted

Oven element is shorted

Wire is burnt off of the oven element and is touching metal

Bad switch or shorted switch

Bare wire is touching metal range

Range is not wired correctly

Dead rodent is laying across hot wire

Tinfoil touching wire oven element

Tinfoil touching burner or drip pan touching wire connection to the burner.

Timer will not work

Clock motor won't run

Motor runs but won't turn the gears

Dial is loose on the shaft

Fuse is blown out

Wire is burnt off the timer switch or a loose connection

Broken gear or shaft

Index

A

AC ammeter, clip-on, 22, 23, 24
Adding refrigerant, 96
Automatic washer pump, 179

B

Bearings, motor, 49, 50
Bell housing, 46
Belt type elements, 226, 227
Brake, automatic washer, 177, 178
Breaker strips, 105
Broil element, range, 277
Burner repair, 270, 271

C

Capacitor checks, 25, 26
Capacitor, motor, 138
Capacitor, motor starting, 124
Capacitor-start motor, 42, 43
Capillary tube, 54, 62
Capillary tube clogging, 95
Capillary tube freeze, 95
Centrifugal switch, motor, 42
Charging refrigerator system, 95
Circulating fan, frost-free refrigerator, 76
Cleaning, dishwasher pump, 155
Clip-on ammeter, 22, 23, 24
Clock motor, timer, 79, 80
Clogged capillary tube, 95
Clogging, disposer, 252, 253

Compressor, refrigeration, 54, 57, 58, 59, 60
Condenser fan motors, 143
Condenser, refrigerator, 54
Continuity check, 21
Continuously variable range switch, 269
"Current" relay, 130
Cycles, automatic washer, 166, 167

D

Defrost timer, 76, 79
Dishwasher door gasket, 156
Dishwasher heating element, 150, 159
"Dividing" the system, refrigerator, 99
Door gasket replacement, 107
Door latches, 103
Door removal, refrigerator, 103
Door switch, drier, 202, 219
"Down 10" transformer, 11
Drain connection, disposer, 249
Drain, dishwasher, 161
Drain, frost-free refrigerator, 72, 73
Drier door switch, 202
Drier installation, 206
Drier, refrigeration system, 96, 97
Drive pulleys, drier, 210
Drum rollers, drier, 202
Dry nitrogen test, 29

E

Elements, water heater, 226
Evaporator, refrigeration, 55, 63

F

Fan, frost-free refrigerator, 76
Fan-type condenser, refrigeration, 62
Faucet connections, dishwasher, 148
Filter, range, 284
Fin-type condenser, refrigeration, 61
Flange, disposer mounting, 243
Flare connection, 32, 34
Freezer door gasket, 107
Freezer unit won't run, 124
Frost-free refrigerator, 70, 71, 72, 74
"Frozen" compressor, 130
Fuse, range, 284
Fusing, water heater, 230

G

Gauges, refrigeration, 87, 88
Gas pressure, measuring, 93
Gas refrigeration, 55
Gasket, door, 107
Grinding, disposer, 252

H

Halide torch, 97
Hammer, disposer, 250
Heater defrost system, 72
Heater element, drier, 215, 216, 217
Heater element switch, drier, 208, 209
Heating element, defrost system, 77, 78

Heating element, dishwasher, 150, 159
Hot gas defrost system, 75, 81
"Hot wire" relay, 130

I

Impeller, dishwasher, 152, 165
Installation, water heater, 229

L

Lamp check, 20, 21
Latches, refrigerator-freezer doors, 103
Leak, valve, 188, 189
Leaks, 97
Leaks, dishwasher, 156
Leaks, refrigeration system, 97
Leaks, refrigerator or freezer, 28
Line voltage level, 7
Line-tap valve, 31
Lint trap, drier, 199, 200, 201
"Low side," refrigeration system, 63
Lubrication, dryer, 212, 213

M

Manual compressor start, 125
Motor bearings, 49, 50
Motor, condenser fan, 143
Motor capacitor checker, 25
Motor, drier, 209
Motor-start switches, 45
Motor starting box, 27, 129
Motor-starting capacitor, 124
Motor-starting relay, dishwasher, 162
Motor-starting relays, refrigeration, 130
Motor troubleshooting chart, 52, 53
Motor winding check, 124

Motor winding resistance, 22
Mounting, disposer, 243

N

Neon test lamp, 8

O

Ohmmeter, 15, 16
Overload, drier, 205
Overload protectors, refrigeration, 136
Overload switch, 122, 123
Oven elements, 274

P

Parallel capacitors, 140
Plug, range, 265
"Potential" relay, 132, 135
Pressure valve, water heater, 230
Pump, automatic washer, 179
Pump, dishwasher, 153

R

Range plug, 265
Range timer, 278
Refrigerant, adding to system, 90
Refrigerant check, 91
Refrigerant, measuring, 94
Refrigeration cycle, 56
Refrigeration gas, 55
Refrigeration gauges, 87, 88
Refrigerator door removal, 110
Refrigerator unit won't run, 122
Relay, dishwasher, motor-starting, 162
Resistance, 16
Resistance, motor windings, 125
Rinse cycle, automatic washer, 178
Run capacitor, 44

"Running" capacitor, motor, 138

S

Safety valve, water heater, 232
Scales, meter, 18
Schraeder valves, 29
Seal, disposer mounting, 243
Series capacitors, 140
Shaded-pole motor, 44
Shunt, ohmmeter, 16
Slip clutch, spin cycle, 176
"Slippage," spin cycle, 175
Slow-blow fuse, 120
Snifter valves, 29
Solenoid valves, 163
Spill-over system, refrigeration, 67, 68, 69
Spin cycle, automatic washer, 167, 175
Split-phase motor, 42
Starter box, 129
Starting relay, refrigeration, 66
Starting switches, motor, 45
Static condenser, refrigeration, 61
"Stuck" compressor, 130
Submersible element, 226, 228
Suction line, refrigeration, 64, 65
"Suds savers," automatic washers, 189, 190
Surface burner, 268
Swaging, 36, 37, 38, 39
Switch, disposer, 247
Switches, oven, 269
Switches, surface burner, 268

T

Temperature selector, drier, 221
Terminals, range, 266
Test lamp, 8, 9
Thermostat, 55
Thermostat, drier, 222

Thermostat, refrigerator, 84, 85, 86, 87
Thermostat, water heater, 232
Thermostatic sensor, range, 269
Thermostats, refrigeration, 143
Timer, automatic washer, 168
Timer, defrost, 76, 79
Timer, dishwasher, 157
Timer, drier, 218
Timer, range, 278
Transformer, line voltage up and down, 12
Transmission, automatic washer, 183
Tubing connection, 32

Vent pipe, drier, 207
Voltage measurements, 19
"Voltage" relay, 130
Volt-Ohmmeter, 17

W

Wash cycle, automatic washer, 166, 175
Washer pump, 179, 180
Water level control, automatic washer, 188
Water valves, automatic washer, 184
Wiring diagram, range, 279
Wiring, dishwasher, 148
Wiring, water heater, 232

V

Valves, water, automatic washer, 184, 185

Z

Zero-adjust, ohmmeter, 16, 17